A NEW EASTER RISING

Paul Reid
with Ruth Morrison

Logikos Christian Publishing

Logikos Christian Publishing
155 Glebe Street
Leigh
Lancs.
WN7 1RH

Copyright © 1993 Paul Reid
ISBN 1 898214 00X

All rights reserved. No part of this publication
may be produced, stored in a retrieval system, or
transmitted, in any form or by any means, electronic,
mechanical, photocopying, recording or otherwise,
without the prior permission of the publisher.

Typeset by Vision Typesetting, Manchester

Printed and bound in Great Britain
by Cox and Wyman Ltd, Reading, Berks.

Cover Design by Vic Mitchell

Dedicated to

JAMES SCOTT

My father-in-law and father in the Lord.
My friend, mentor and supporter.

Acknowledgements

I wish to thank Linda Thompson for all her hard work, and also Dr. John Kelly for his valuable contribution.

My thanks are also due to Ruth Morrison, without whose work this book would not have been written. Finally, thanks to my wife Priscilla, whose love and patience have kept me on course. You taught me through your life to worship the Father, love the Son, and be guided by the Holy Spirit in a way I never dreamed possible. Still my lover and my best friend after seventeen years.

Paul Reid
Belfast, 1993

Foreword

With tears in his eyes, the manager of the holiday camp at Mosney, in Southern Ireland, told how his sick friend had spoken of Jesus walking through the streets of Mosney. 'This has happened this week,' the manager added emotionally. The week to which he referred was the 'Together for the Kingdom' week, largely a result of Paul Reid and a few others whose inspiration, faith and drive brought this unusual gathering together in 1992.

I had been given the privilege of addressing the last meeting of this historic conference, made up of Christians of all denominations from Northern and Southern Ireland. In a society weary of violence and sectarian division, the atmosphere of love, joy and peace which pervaded the Christian convention was an evidence of the presence of God's Holy Spirit. The experience of unity which was shared in that time was

FOREWORD

made possible only by Jesus Christ who prayed that we 'should be one'.

This achievement alone would be enough to commend Paul and his story to a potential reader. However, there's a lot more also to be said. I have known Paul for over twenty years – in fact more precisely since the day he drove me to the airport after I'd completed an evangelistic mission at Queen's University, Belfast. His willingness to serve, his hunger for God, his spiritual leadership and effective guidance of the Christian Fellowship Church in Belfast, gives us a story full of practical wisdom and encouragement for our own walk with God.

C.F.C. is one of the many new churches which have sprung up in the United Kingdom, demonstrating that Christianity is still virile, even in war-torn Northern Ireland, but virile with love and truth rather than with the much publicised violence. The variety that always comes from the Holy Spirit is expressed in these many new churches, with their different expressions showing a Christianity alive and well. However, this kind of Christianity needs a type of leadership which is not merely a bureaucratic holding operation. When the wind of the Spirit fills the sails of the church, inspiring men and women of God are needed at the helm in order to steer God's people through the vicissitudes of violence, suffering, pain and sectarianism such as is found in Belfast and Northern Ireland.

I was present when the original leadership of C.F.C. resigned, and the whole weight and response of the C.F.C. membership for whom they had been responsible fell upon Paul. The sensitivity with which he sought God's face, counsel from others, and the subsequent rising to this responsibility evidenced a man upon whom God's hand had been at work, preparing him for such a time as this. Indeed a man for such a time as Ireland needs at this hour, who will serve and labour together with others in the love of Christ and the power of the Spirit, and who are searching to bring, as Jeremiah says, a future and a hope for this people.

Will you pray with me for Paul as you read his story? Pray also that God will raise up others like him, in order that He may bring His unique and only realistic solution for this province of the United Kingdom. Some of us believe that the raising up of men like Paul for this time is already an answer for those who have been crying to God that His will would be done in this situation which seems to have no ultimate solution. If you've not prayed for such before, I trust this book will help you to begin. So let's begin . . .

Roger Forster
London, 1993

Preface

On a daily basis, Roman Catholics and Protestants murder one another on the city streets and in the rural areas of Northern Ireland. 'Tit for tat' killings are carried out by paramilitaries, in spite of constant appeals for no retaliation by heartbroken widows and orphans. In inner city Belfast, ghettos and 'no go' areas now exist where formerly people lived alongside neighbours of a different religious persuasion. There are those who believe that we are closer to an all-out war situation than we have ever been.

Even the Church is divided. Many preach a gospel of love, but seem unable to shake off the labels of Orange and Green. In the eighties, a young Presbyterian minister in the north west of the province, was driven out of the country because he dared to cross the road to extend the season's greetings to a neighbouring Roman Catholic congregation on Christmas Day.

PREFACE

There have been many movements for peace over the troubled decades, since the turbulent People's Democracy marches and the introduction of the British army onto streets in Northern Ireland in 1969–70, sparked off the present period of political unrest. Christians have cried out to God to heal our nation and God is answering, not by changing structures, but by changing hearts. Roman Catholics and Protestants are coming together, not simply in an effort to understand one another, but in united recognition that there is a fresh move of the Holy Spirit, bringing repentance and reconciliation under the banner of the kingdom of God.

At Easter 1992, 2,500 Christians gathered for a week's nationwide conference at the Mosney holiday camp in the south of Ireland. Believers from as far apart as Cork and Coleraine travelled to celebrate new life in Christ. They came from every denominational background to worship, study, and fellowship together in the first event of its kind in Ireland.

Together for the Kingdom, is this decade's attempt to bridge the gap between Roman Catholic and Protestant in a united stand in Ireland. It is a major shift historically as the first national gathering organized by New Church leaders, north and south, who have a vision for non-sectarian Christianity. At the 1993 conference, we hope to build on the foundation already laid, and spread the vision for new churches springing up through the length and breadth of Ireland, with a message of peace and hope.

In 1992, a significant moment came right at the end

of the conference week. During the final evening celebration, Phelim McClosky, owner and managing director of the Mosney complex, was invited onto the platform so that we could publicly express our gratitude for his co-operation. He was accompanied by two of his senior managers. After receiving our thanks, he moved forward to the microphone to recount an incident which had occurred shortly after he had purchased the Mosney site. He and a friend were walking down the main street of the camp, when his companion suddenly remarked, 'Phelim, one day Jesus will come to Mosney.' As he related this Phelim paused, then said, 'I believe that happened this week.' This prophetic statement from a man who admitted that he was not himself religious, was followed by an awed silence and then a spontaneous burst of applause. Jesus was indeed at Mosney in 1992. There were many witnesses to His power to transform and restore broken lives and broken relationships. Men and women met Him for the first time, and others experienced a fresh anointing of the Holy Spirit.

I stood on the same platform that night and marvelled at the work of God in my life which had brought me there. I had been broken and changed by the power of the Holy Spirit from a narrow minded, self-righteous northern evangelical, into a servant of God's desire for repentance and restoration among His people throughout the whole island. Many of us at Mosney had been through a similar process, whereby God had demolished strongholds in our lives, and led us to a place of faith where we could claim His promise together, '... if my people, who are called by my name, will humble themselves and pray and seek my face and turn from their wicked ways, then will I hear from heaven and will forgive their sin and will heal their land.' (2 Chronicles 7:14)

1
In The Meetings

It was six o'clock in the evening. Priscilla was clearing away the tea things, Deborah and Lucy had settled down to homeworks and Susan and Amy were yelling and screaming upstairs. The signature tune of our favourite soap, Neighbours, was blaring in the background, and as I got up to investigate what my two youngest daughters were doing, the telephone rang.

I lifted the receiver and a stranger's voice spoke, 'Hello Paul, it's your dad.' For a moment I could not reply, I had not heard from this man for nineteen years. He knew nothing about my life and I did not even know where he was living. Now here he was on the other end of the line. I managed a few pleasantries. He then he asked me what I was doing and I told him that I was the leader of a large Belfast church. He was astounded, and talked briefly about his own life. He was semi-retired from his job as a salesman, and had two daughters by his new wife. He gave me his address and asked me to give a copy to my sister, Linda, and with that he was gone.

My emotions were in turmoil. Painful memories came flooding back and I wondered if I had done the right thing in contacting him after all these years. A week earlier he had turned sixty. I knew his birthday and believed that in response to all God was doing in my life, I should write to him. The letter was straightforward and to the point. I sent him best wishes on the occasion of his birthday, and then went on to tell him that as I had received God's forgiveness through Jesus Christ, I wanted him to know that I had forgiven him for all the pain he had caused in my life. Furthermore I asked him to forgive me for the bitterness I had harboured against him.

I did not know how to get the letter to him. The address my mother had was out-of-date, so I contacted the English court where the initial maintenance order had been taken out. They refused to tell me where he was living, but promised that if I sent the letter to them under separate cover, they would forward it. Now a week later, he had responded with a phone call. Moreover he said that he wanted to keep in touch. My mind went back to an encounter in an hotel room in Henley-on-Thames where my father had been stationed with the Royal Air Force. I had gone with my mother to appeal to him to come home. There was an emotional scene where he shouted and both my mother and I wept. I remember on that occasion begging my father not to leave us.

IN THE MEETINGS

Since the first phonecall five years ago, my father and I have kept in touch, mostly at my initiative. During one such call, my daughter, Deborah, was listening on the other line and she was horrified to discover that he knew neither my age nor my date of birth. Once I asked him why he had never made any attempt to get in touch with us over all the years. He had moved house and we had no idea where he was. His reply was pathetic in its simplicity, 'I didn't know what to say.' I told my sister that I had renewed contact with our father, but she did not want a copy of his address. For her the pain was as deep as ever.

Linda and I were together when we last saw our father. He had stayed in England after leaving the R.A.F. It was September 1969, and my mother was making a final attempt to save her marriage. I was eighteen and I felt numb as I watched my mother and sister crying in the street outside his home in Southend-on-Sea, where he was living with his new family. Mother knocked the neighbours up when my father refused her entry, shouting 'This man is married to me!' She accused him of threatening her, and he and I almost came to blows. It was quite easily the most awful experience of my life. Eventually I dragged my mother and Linda away. We had brought Linda in an attempt to induce remorse, but my father had chosen a new life and I could see we were not wanted. It was time to go home and try to patch up our lives. I have not seen him since that day. Five years later my parents divorced. We went out for a celebration meal, but it was hollow. My father's desertion of our family left deep scars in all our lives.

The summer of 1967 was a crazy, rebellious time. I was living with my mother, half-brother Raymond and my sister, Linda in my grandparents' home in Carryduff. Mother was suffering the trauma of her marriage breakdown, and she just couldn't cope. During my father's career in the R.A.F., he had been posted to Singapore. My mother went with him and I was sent as a boarder to Methodist College in Belfast. At 'Methody,' I had quickly grown very independent, and it was difficult now to readjust to family life, especially without a father.

I spent the summer weeks hell-raising; I was often drunk and defied any attempts at control. Linda was only fifteen months younger, and there developed a close bond between us. At times my mother complained that we ganged up on her, but Linda's allegiance to me was natural in the absence of a father, whom she greatly missed. We got involved in all our youthful rebellions together.

I was an angry teenager with a strong sense of rejection. My two main interests were girls and football. As a loyal Linfield supporter, I cheered from the stands fifty-two times a season. We had always plenty of money and I became very self-assured. I also had the advantage of size. At the age of twelve my passport records that I was 5'5ins., and two years later I was 6'2ins. I had to carry identification for half-fare on the bus, but I was able to get in to the pictures to see 18-rated films from the age of thirteen. One Wednesday afternoon, I mitched off games and went to the Ritz to see Stewart Grainger in Sodom and Gomorrah. When the lights came up, I discovered Raymond, my half-brother, sitting in the same row. I was surprised to see him, not simply because he was at Queen's and should have been attending lectures, but because he had recently announced that he had become a Christian. In Northern Ireland a born-again Christian does not go to the cinema, so I said, 'I thought you were saved.' Embarrassed, he replied, 'So did I!' Both sets of grandparents were founder members of Plymouth Brethren assemblies. My mother is a professing Christian, and her parents, Thomas and Lilly Lowe, were important influences throughout those teenage years. My grandfather was a wealthy man. During his time as a building contractor in Carryduff, he employed nearly every man in the townland. The local bus stop was known as Lowe's corner. One stipulation made by Thomas Lowe was that all members of his household would attend the Sunday night gospel meeting.

For the sake of a quiet life, Linda and I went along every Sunday night, but we had little respect for what happened there. We amused ourselves by flicking pieces of paper into my grandfather's hat and passing mint imperials up and down the row. There were times, however, when I resolved to talk to Linda about us 'getting saved,' but as in the parable of the sower, the ground was hard and the seed was quickly snatched away.

As a youth, my greatest fear was that Jesus would come back and I would not be ready. In June 1967, the six day Arab-Israeli war made a great impact on me. I had heard enough about the end times to be afraid that these 'signs' might indicate the Lord's imminent return. In the autumn after my summer of rebellion, my great uncle, Hugh Lyndsay, invited me to a series of meetings held in a local country village. Drumaness was 99% Roman Catholic, yet it had a Brethren hall. My uncle originally had meetings in a school classroom, and as people got converted, he started an assembly. The mission was conducted by Noel Lowden and Bobby Neill. I went to the meetings every night for a week, and from the first night, I knew that this was the time to get my life sorted out.

For two days I prepared to face up to the call of God. On the Wednesday afternoon, I sat in the park smoking. As I threw the butt in the bin, I said to myself, 'That's my last cigarette.' Later in the meeting, Noel Lowden preached on Romans 10:9, '... if you confess with your mouth, Jesus is Lord, and believe in your heart that God raised him from the dead, you will be saved.' There was no appeal and no emotion, but that night I met Jesus and for the first time truly confessed Him as Lord. It was 25th October 1967. I was sixteen and I had stopped running. My father was not coming back, but Jesus had broken into my life and began to reveal to me the father heart of God. My brother Raymond, six years my senior, became a Christian ten days later. After several 'failed' attempts he had finally found the Lord, and we embarked on our journey of faith together. At the end of November, we were both baptized in Knockbracken Gospel Hall.

I immediately announced the fact that I had been 'born again' to my shocked school friends, and earned for myself the nickname, Billy Graham. The teachers soon found out that Reid had 'got religious,' because mine was a radical conversion. Gone were the smoking, drinking and bad language. My life totally changed and the kingdom of God became my passion. At school, I was a keen member of the Dramatic and Debating Societies. I enjoyed addressing an audience and once, while on a Scripture Union holiday to Capernwray Hall, a teacher predicted that I would make a good preacher some day. I had a shaky start, however, when asked to give my testimony for the first time. I prepared well, and rehearsed in front of the mirror. I even recorded my talk on tape and it was to last an epic forty-seven minutes. In the event, however, I dried up after just two minutes, and stood in agony a full minute more before sitting down. Red in the face and perspiring heavily I vowed, 'never again!' My family was delighted at my conversion. This was the year of angry exchanges between my parents, but my father did express satisfaction at the news of my reformation. Eager to encourage me in spiritual matters, my aunt invited me to a Bible class. The main attraction, however, was a beautiful girl called Priscilla Scott, who wore a brace. Undeterred, I asked her out just before her fifteenth birthday and, in spite of counsel against me, she agreed.

Priscilla's long-suffering family was to become one of the greatest influences in my life. Her parents, Jim and Lil, were also in the Brethren, and I began to join them going to the meetings. I remember on one occasion travelling in the car with Priscilla, her parents and her brother and sister, and they were all singing choruses. Something of the warmth of togetherness touched me. I wept when I went home and cried to the Lord, 'Why couldn't I have had a family like that?' There was still a hurting little boy inside this tall young man, and it was years before I could allow God to begin to heal the pain.

I did fairly well at school in the Arts subjects I liked and even received a prize the year I became a Christian, but I felt increasing pressure to be the 'man about the house.' I left school, therefore, after completing 'O' levels, and it was a natural step to follow my mother and grandmother into the world of business. My aunt owned a shop in Belfast city centre. She gave me a start in the clothing trade, and I began to sell for a manufacturer's agent. Initially my brother drove, as we travelled round shops and took orders. Soon my grandfather bought me a car, and by the time I was given the agency in 1969, I was earning six thousand pounds a year.

I enjoyed selling. I loved the thrill of carrying £500 in my pocket and, although I was still young, I lived the life of a successful entrepreneur. As well as having other agencies, I worked for the biggest corsetry firm in Europe, which led to the accusation that, 'Paul Reid travels in ladies' underwear.' Making money was always an important feature in my family's life, and I was fairly good at it.

IN THE MEETINGS

At one stage, I visited almost every retail outlet of ladies' clothing in N.Ireland. I was often asked by fellow businessmen if I was in the 'Mafia.' I discoverd that this meant was I 'in the meetings' ie. a full member of a Brethren assembly. I had been accepted into membership in Knockbracken Gospel Hall, and had quickly grasped all the do's and don'ts of Christianity, Brethren-style. I threw myself into church life and became a Sunday School teacher. A parent once commented that her son, 'laughed a lot and learned a little.' A significant figure in my life at that time, was Brian Tatford, a missionary on furlough from France, who led a series of meetings in Apsley Street Gospel Hall. These were held after the Sunday night service and included practical Christian teaching, of a kind unknown in Brethren assemblies. It was less than a year since my conversion, and I was happy to know that I was 'saved' and going to heaven. Brian Tatford preached on the lordship of Christ and said that during Jesus' ministry on earth, people accepted him as Lord first and then Saviour, not the other way round. God spoke powerfully to me, and in a fresh way I understood that He was in complete control of my life. For the first time Priscilla and I wept about spiritual things.

As a young Christan, I began preaching almost immediately. The Brethren assemblies have an unstructured, but very definite, discipleship scheme. An older man takes a younger man under his wing, and I was blessed in this regard to come to the attention of Jim Scott, Priscilla's father. We travelled to many meetings together. As the junior partner, I read out the hymns and intimations, and gave my testimony. Jim then taught from the Word. As time progressed and we were invited to return to particular assemblies, I began to do some preaching.

I am grateful for the wise, godly counsel received from Jim Scott during those formative years. His fatherly love and prayers were vital to my spiritual growth. He had suffered much rejection in his own life, but God had turned that into amazing compassion for others. He was, and is, such an encourager, and I always felt completely accepted by him. Those years on the road with Jimmy, were my Bible college training. I learned so much from hearing him preach and observing his walk with the Lord. Then there were the practical tips, 'Prepare plenty of material,' 'If you get stuck give your testimony,' 'It's a good thing to finish on a verse.' In time I was no longer the disciple, and I took younger men along with me, but Jim Scott has remained one of my greatest supporters to this day.

It was the early seventies, the age of side locks, long hair and kipper ties. I was conservative by most standards, but I did wear my hair slightly over the tops of my ears. On one occasion, Jim and I were invited to speak at an assembly in Wallace Avenue, Lisburn. We were sitting in an ante-room waiting for the prayer meeting to start, when an elderly man addressed me, 'You're not preaching here tonight are you?' His tone was aggressive, but I hesitantly said, 'Yes.' 'Not with hair like that you're not!' he replied. I protested that I had visited the barber's the week before, but he only retorted, 'You might have been to the barber's, but you didn't get your hair cut.' When eventually I did begin to preach that evening, the brother who was offended by my appearance, sat with his head in his Bible, and read.

We truly believed that the Brethren were the sole custodians of the truth. Occasionally we came across ministers from other denominations at funerals, and we seriously doubted their salvation. When invited to speak at a Presbyterian Sunday service, I refused. Their doctrinal emphasis and differing practices led me to question whether it was really 'church.' In the outworking of our faith, the essential elements included the absence of music and clergy, the leading of the Holy Spirit in the meetings, an insistence on the women wearing hats and taking no active part, and the centrality of Scripture and the Breaking of Bread. I was at home in this environment, and could not foresee the time when I would have to consider alternatives.

On the political front, the present 'Troubles' were beginning to grip the Northern Ireland communities. Although brought up in the Protestant tradition, I was decidedly apolitical. This was largely owing to the influence of the Brethren, who did not involve themselves in party politics, and did not vote. They hold strongly to the belief that, as Christians, our citizenship is in heaven; we are here as ambassadors from a foreign country, to represent our head of government. It is of no consequence if you are Orange or Green, take communion every Sunday, have been baptized in your local church, or go to confession regularly – 'If you're not born again, you're not saved!' At school my best friend was a Roman Catholic. John McDonagh's mother was Belgian and his father was an English army sergeant, stationed at the barracks on the Holywood Road. John came with us to the Linfield matches and sang all the 'kick the Pope' songs, which are an essential feature of supporting that particular Belfast team. The repartee was without bitterness. Indeed when I studied Irish history, I had quite romantic notions about the I.R.A., and wondered if a united Ireland wouldn't be the best thing. Sectarian violence had not yet reared its ugly head in our lives.

Priscilla's family was soon to become mine and theirs was my second home. I was best man at the wedding of her sister Vivien to my good friend, Les McKeown. In 1982, his sister, Karen, was leaving Albertbridge Congregational Church when she was shot in the back of the neck by an I.N.L.A. gunman. She was immediately paralyzed and died three weeks later. It was a totally sectarian attack; Karen was in the wrong place at the wrong time. She was a lovely Christian girl, only twenty. I shared in the family's grief and learned that a young man growing up in Northern Ireland, could not ignore the divisions. It was several years, however, before I began to ask whether Christians could be part of the solution, as religion was so clearly at the heart of the problem.

In the meantime, I was doing very well in a good job

with excellent prospects. I was the grandson of Thomas Lowe and, like him, believed that there was nothing I could not achieve with hard work and application. I was settled in the Brethren, where I was gaining a clear understanding of biblical doctrine. I believed that I knew everything there was to know about being a Christian, and that all that remained was to preach the message of the gospel to the 'lost.' I was strong-willed, forceful and opinionated. But God had not finished with me, and he began to challenge my pride and arrogance.

My sister, Linda, came to know the Lord shortly after I did. After leaving school, she decided that she wanted to go on a missionary venture to Morocco with an organisation called, Youth with a Mission. I was enjoying success in my business at that time, and I was happy to finance the trip. While there, she became friendly with a young German man. They met up again a few months later in Spain, and when she returned home, Lothar Schulz came too.

Linda was an eighteen-year-old university student with the opportunity to pursue a career in Pharmacy ahead of her, but when Lothar moved in with us in May, they immediately began to make plans to marry in the summer of the same year. They were full of 'new' teachings, and they started to try and persuade me of the importance of the baptism in the Holy Spirit. Linda was convinced about this and was equally stubborn on the question of her wedding. All attempts by me and my mother to encourage them to wait failed, and for a while our relationship was strained. However, I had lost my father and did not want to lose my only sister, so when they were married as planned, it was with our blessing.

Lothar and Linda lived with several Christian families before settling in a community at Cotton Mount, Mallusk. Linda left university after one year, in order to start a family. I disapproved of their relaxed lifestyle and their emphasis on the Holy Spirit and speaking in tongues. However, although I cared little for his 'new' ideas, I was greatly troubled by the refusal of the local elders to allow Lothar to 'break bread' in our assembly. I came close to leaving over this issue, but was calmed by the more tolerant attitude of Jim Scott, who was prepared to accept any brother in the Lord at the 'table.' I stayed in the Brethren, but I began to recognize God at work outside the confines of the assemblies. This happened mainly through Priscilla. She left school with very good grades, but chose to go to work in the Library Service, in order to help her family. After one year, she was sponsored by the Education and Library Board to take a diploma in Library Studies at Queen's University. This was then extended to four years so that she could obtain her degree. It was a real blessing that she was able to study with full pay. At Queen's, Priscilla was moving in new circles, and came into contact with believers from other churches, through her involvement in the Christian Union. She was elected on to the executive committee, and I began to accompany her to meetings, where we made many good friends. John Thompson and Ian Mitchell, both

Presbyterians, were later to serve the Lord alongside me in C.F.C. I was being forced to the conclusion that you didn't have to be in the Brethren to be a genuine Christian!

2

Beyond the Brethren

Those were the days of a movement of the Holy Spirit in Northern Ireland, with the visit from the U.S.A. of the band, Liberation Suite, and the musical, Come Together, written by Carol and Jamie Owens, starring Pat Boone. I went to Come Together, but I was so horrified that I walked out. I was embarrassed by the emotional singing and the hands waving in the air.

The whole thing was beyond my comprehension and therefore, I decided, unbiblical. Pat Boone invited us to give a 'clap offering' to the Lord, and as if that wasn't enough, we were then encouraged to hug someone we didn't know. I nearly passed out. There were several Roman Catholic nuns sitting nearby and I thought, 'If a nun comes and hugs me, I will die!' That was when I left the meeting; at least in the Brethren you knew where you were.

In the early seventies, the biggest thing among

A NEW EASTER RISING

Brethren assemblies was Brooklands Gospel Hall. Originally a temporary wooden structure, it was situated in a Protestant working-class estate in the Belfast suburb of Dundonald. Drew Craig was a forward thinking man with a heart after God and a desire to present the gospel in a way which was relevant to modern society. He gathered a group of like-minded people around him, including Ian and Avril Barr and Clifford and Heather Kennedy, with whom I was to work years later.

Coffee-bars were all the rage then, primarily as a means of reaching young people, and Drew invited me to speak. Brooklands was Brethren, but it remained 'different' for some years. I couldn't explain it at the time, but when I preached there on the first and many subsequent occasions, I enjoyed a fresh anointing and felt something stir in my spirit, a foretaste of things to come.

One feature of life at Brooklands was the summer camp. In 1975 I went with a crowd of young people to a centre in North Wales. The camp was led by Ian Barr, and I was the speaker or 'padre.' It was a tremendous time. I was faced with many questions from young people of very different backgrounds. One earnest Brethren girl was concerned because she was not looking forward to the Lord's return with any enthusiasm, while a lad from the estate tackled me during the ferry crossing about my views on sexual temptations. In the assembly we were not encouraged to have, never mind express views on such matters! At Brooklands, I had my first experiences of seeing people reached for the Lord. The key was in the life and witness of Drew Craig. He loved the Lord and had a passion for souls. He expected God to work. This had a profound influence on me and as a young man still in my early twenties, I looked to him as a role model. Drew was causing ripples in the Brethren community, however, by trying to sacrifice their 'sacred cows.' At the annual Easter conference in Belfast, he publicly questioned the continued use of archaic language. He quoted a phrase, much loved by Brethren preachers, 'Christ died in our guilty room and stead,' and admitted that for years he had thought this meant 'bed and breakfast.' It was a red letter day for Drew, and his health suffered as a result of the repercussions.

In 1975, when Priscilla graduated, we were married. We bought a house in Carryduff near to where my mother was living, and became active members of Knockbracken Gospel Hall. We had a burden for young people, and for nearly seven years we ran a children's meeting in the assembly and a coffee-bar in an old barn outside Carryduff. The Loft coffee-bar drew a mixed crowd of young people from miles around, and we held a Bible Study in conjunction with it. We loved the Brethren, but our hearts and minds were being opened up to see God at work in a broader context.

We read about a Christian conference in Buzz magazine, and in 1979 we went to the first Spring Harvest. We took our new baby daughter, Deborah, and Priscilla's brother, Andrew, then fourteen. Spring

Harvest blew our minds! There we were exposed to new teaching and a totally different form of worship. God began to turn our lives around. Luis Palau was the main speaker and Ian Barclay, an Anglican cleric, did the Bible readings on the book of Daniel. Both were truly inspiring. The theme of the conference was, 'Making an impact where you live.' It was a place of new beginnings. We met people like Clive Calver and Peter Meadows, founder and editor of Buzz, friends to this day. We got a fresh vision for evangelism among adults, and we returned home to the little backwater of Carryduff, determined to make an impact there for God.

The Loft died a natural death when the barn we were using was demolished. Campbell Emerson, who owned a car showroom in the town, agreed to let us use adjacent function rooms, known as the Dogwood Rooms, for outreach meetings. Our aim was to attract people with no church connections, so with the help of a few friends, we started an after-church rally on alternate Sundays. We served tea and coffee, introduced a bookstall and piano, and did not insist on women wearing hats. All pretty tame by today's standards, but innovative in the Carryduff of the late seventies. I was preaching the gospel and we believed that God was going to do great things, but He didn't.

Joe Bailie, an elder in the Meeting House in Randalstown, took an interest in our outreach activities. One day he asked me what I would do if six people were saved at the next meeting. I replied that I would send them to the local Baptist church, because taking young people to the Brethren would be like taking your granny to a disco! Slowly the light began to dawn, and I found myself questioning my allegiance to the assembly. We had begun to reach out to folks in the area, but felt weighed down at times by the trappings of religion. A gap was developing between us and our Brethren friends and we began to seek the Lord. I recall crying out to the Lord, 'If this is abundant life, we're all in big trouble!' For two years a small group of us prayed fervently that God would revive the Brethren. We had no desire to leave, but what we were doing did not meet with the approval of the local assembly, nor was it doing the job. We had a piano and lively singing, but we were not seeing people converted. What more did we need? We recognized the void in our lives that no amout of Christian activity was able to fill. I think I knew then that we needed an outpouring of the Holy Spirit, but I saw the Charismatic Movement as too great a threat to my Brethren identity to pursue the matter at that time.

In my distress I cried out to God, and He answered with a question. 'Paul, are you open to whatever I ask you to do?' I said 'Yes', and it was a breakthrough day for me, but when I told Priscilla that I meant it, even if God asked me to join the local Presbyterians, she thought I was 'off my trolley.' She believed that doing anything for God could only mean moving elsewhere within Brethren assemblies. How could I change so much, I who embarrassed her in front of her Presbyterian friends because of my strong convictions about believer's baptism? It was in this great confusion of mind and spirit, that we returned to Spring Harvest in 1981, this time with a second baby on the way. We were desperately looking for guidance, praying and seeking God. For five days heaven seemed closed - nothing from God. Then on the final night David Pawson spoke from Deuteronomy Ch. 1, 'You have stayed long enough at this mountain;...' vs.6 This was a prophetic word to us. God was again challenging my willingness to obey Him as He led me forward into new things.

That night Priscilla and I both heard God's call to move on, but I fidgeted so much during the meeting that she was afraid I hadn't got the message. As David Pawson developed his sermon, he drew attention to Jethro's warning to Moses about the dangers of one man ministry. He emphasized the importance of exercising gifts within the Body, and challenged those to whom God was speaking to stand up. For the first time I responded publicly to an appeal, and Priscilla and I stood together. The speaker was asking for those whom God was calling into leadership, to take a step of faith and believe that He would fulfil His purposes in their lives. As the meeting closed, those who had responded were ushered into the conference table-tennis room. There were at least three hundred of us, too many for him to deal with individually, so David Pawson asked us to turn to the person next to us, find out who he or she was, offer some advice and take our first steps in leadership. I talked to a man, also from a Brethren assembly, who asked me what I was going to do. Without hesitation I replied, 'I am going to leave and start a church.' I had not talked to Priscilla about this, but that night we both heard the same word from God, and I was speaking in faith what I could hardly contemplate. As we returned home, we knew that something significant had happened in our lives, which was to have far-reaching consequences.

We played the tape of the final meeting to the friends who worked with us in the Dogwood Rooms, and we told them that whatever their convictions, we were leaving the Gospel Hall. I went to see the assembly elders, led by Samuel Thompson, a cousin of my mother's, and including Jim Scott, my father-in-law, to tell them of our plans to start meeting on our own. I was naive enough to expect their support, but they were shell-shocked. They asked if we would still be Brethren, but I said that I didn't think so.

I saw it as a question of obedience. I did not know what lay ahead, but I was sure that God was asking us to leave. Not even the elders' offer to get an organ could have persuaded me to stay. I said I would go when there were ten of us and this came very soon, but not before we were accused of being divisive by friends who had been with us in the children's work. This was very hurtful coming from people whom we loved. Anxious to be sure that we had heard from God, I asked Him to confirm His will within twenty-four hours.

Travelling home from Coleraine the next night, I stopped off in Randalstown. Joe Bailie had moved to

England and I did not have his address. I knew where evangelist and leader of the Meeting House, George Bates, lived, so I called there to ask for news of Joe. He invited me in and we got talking. When I introduced myself, he surprised me by saying that God had told him I was coming. He had awakened him at four o'clock in the morning to give him a prophetic word for me. He said God wanted to assure me that the path I had chosen was the right one. I was not to hesitate, but go forward with this promise for my situation, 'Trust in the Lord with all your heart and lean not on your own understanding. In all your ways acknowledge Him, and He will direct your paths.' (Proverbs 3:5&6) I stood in the kitchen of George's house, really choked up. God could not have spoken more clearly. Now there was no turning back. As I said goodbye to many years in the Brethren, it was with a deep sadness. I loved and respected those men of God, who by their prayers and example, had nurtured and encouraged me. I regretted the pain caused to anyone, especially Priscilla's parents. We too were hurt by those in the Brethren community who cancelled my speaking engagements in the next few months. It seemed I was no longer welcome in the assemblies because I had left the fold. People soon began to talk about me as if I was dead, 'Paul was a nice fellow.' I experienced a sense of rejection as one person after another withdrew friendship, but I knew that for me a new chapter with the Lord had begun, and I didn't want to miss any of it.

From the first Sunday in September 1981, eleven of

us began to meet in our home, and at the age of thirty, I became the leader of a church. The only way to leave the Brethren was to be more 'right' than the Brethren, so we decided to have no name. We recognized that we were not the only Christians, but believed ourselves to be 'Christians only.' The women participated in the meetings, but wore head coverings as a sign of authority. We believed that we were a New Testament church, practising New Testament principles. I preached every Sunday and rose before 5 a.m. to prepare.

By this time, Priscilla and I had a second daughter, Lucy. As a growing family we started to struggle financially. I was devoting so much time to pastoral care of the members of the fellowship, that I was not putting enough hours into the business. Bad management of funds led to tax bills catching up with us, and by the next summer there was no money to pay for a holiday we had booked in Jersey. Furthermore I owed £5000 to creditors and was overdrawn by the same amount at the bank. Jumping quickly from the red into the black had been no problem in the past, I just put in the extra hours, but now the kingdom of God was taking priority in my time. I had not yet learned how to let God manage every area of my life. He is gracious, however, and often delivers us from problems of our own making.

Around this time I went to the butcher's shop to buy a piece of liver, with only one pound in my pocket. Without explanation, he gave me the meat as a gift, and as I returned home God spoke to me, 'If I can make an ungodly man supply your needs, don't worry about anything.' Later that evening, a promise came to Priscilla, 'My God shall supply all your needs.' The next day a friend from the fellowship arrived at our house with a cheque for £750, exactly the amount required to pay for the holiday! We were learning how to live by faith in God, and in committed family relationship with one another. Community living was big on our agenda as we began to serve one another in love. We had tried the direct approach of evangelism in Carryduff to no avail, so now we concentrated on living lives of love, that others might know that we were the Lord's disciples. For almost a year we enjoyed a close fellowship never experienced by us before. We studied God's Word together, ate together, laughed and cried together and grew together in the Lord. During this time new people joined us and they always brought with them a freshness. We thought we were the only non-charismatic house church in the world.

We decided to go away together for a week-end to Glenada House in Newcastle. During the week-end, we had some major personal disagreements and tempers became very heated. This resulted in great brokenness before the Lord, as we saw our self-centeredness and realized that we were not as 'nice' a group of people as we had thought. As we cried and prayed through the night together, Yvonne Knox shared a verse, which God had impressed on her in preparation for the conference, 'See I am doing a new thing! Now it springs up; do you not perceive it? I am making a way in the desert and streams in the wasteland...' (Isaiah 43:19) God began to bring about a new honesty in our relationships, and I learned a very important truth. When people come together out of rebellion, that same rebellion can prevent them from going forward. It had to be broken in our lives before we could understand that we had not left the Brethren to stagnate in our pride. We had embarked on a journey, and it had only just begun.

3

Oh no, not tongues!

God was gradually expanding my vision. In the early days of the fellowship, He spoke to me about 'taking the land' for His kingdom. When my grandfather, Thomas Lowe, died in 1976, I inherited a quarter share in a plot of land in Carryduff. My grandmother, who died some years previously, had cherished the dream of a Gospel Hall being built on this land. Could God be calling us to establish a more visible witness in the town? Eventually my mother and aunt sold their shares, and I became joint owner with my brother Raymond, who at that time was attending the meetings in our house.

All along I resisted pressure to have permanent premises for the fellowship, believing that it might destroy what God was doing through relationships. God spoke to me again, and I began to see 'the land,' not simply in terms of a building site, but embracing all of Carryduff and its environs. The revelation was from God, but He had not yet given me the means to interpret and apply His word correctly. It was, therefore, several years before my eyes were opened to see God's plan in terms of the whole island. In the meantime, Carryduff would have to wait for its new hall.

As the leader of a small breakaway group, I knew very little about other fellowships meeting in the province at that time. George Lowden, designer of the Lowden guitar, whom I had led to the Lord, invited me to a conference being held by Bangor Christian Trust, in 1981. Derek Prince was an influential figure in the shaping of the Trust, and he was the speaker at the conference.

I went to one meeting which was significant for me because the leader, John Kelly, gave a message in tongues. It was immediately interpreted, and I was mesmerized. Prior to this, I had thought that tongues did not amount to much more than someone in the next seat mumbling, 'I'll have a Shandy,' but this was different. John spoke with diction and authority, furthermore his prayer language had structure. I remember coming home to Priscilla and conceding, 'I still don't believe it's right, but if I did, I'm sure that's what it would sound like.' The experience had made an impact on me and in the fellowship we embarked on a study of 1 Corinthians. We battled our way through head coverings, again, and came to the end of chapter eleven the week before Spring Harvest 1983. It was a different Paul Reid who was to complete the study.

OH NO, NOT TONGUES!

Spring Harvest had been a vehicle for change in my life before, so I was looking forward to the conference with excited anticipation. Some days before we were due to leave, I awakened in the night with a most strange sensation in my stomach. It felt like something bubbling up inside me, and I thought of Jesus' promise regarding the Holy Spirit, 'Whoever believes in me ... streams of living water will flow from within him.' (John 7:38) I believed that God was preparing me for a fresh encounter with Him at Spring Harvest.

Twelve of us from the fellowship went to the conference. Clifford Edgar and I decided to go to a seminar on the anointing of the Holy Spirit. It was mid-morning, snow was beginning to fall outside, our feet were frozen and there was an irritating echo from the adjoining tent – hardly an atmosphere conducive to spiritual experience! Rob White, from British Youth For Christ, spoke and by way of introduction warned us not to get distracted by terminology and miss the signposts.

He then told his own story, describing himself during his early Christian experience as, 'Brethren and proud of it.' He painted an all-too-familiar picture of reformed self-righteousness. Suddenly God was speaking to my own proud, stubborn heart, and I began to weep. The speaker then went on to give an account of his fierce resistance to the work of the Holy Spirit. He told of how he had worked as a manager in a major department store in the south of England. The doorman was a converted gypsy whose life impressed Rob, but pride caused him to preach doctrine to someone, who although his faith was simple, had something he didn't. Finally Rob humbled himself and asked the doorman to pray with him. 'Nothing dramatic happened,' he said, 'but my life changed.' At the close of the meeting, Rob appealed for those to whom God had been speaking to stand. He strummed quietly on his guitar and encouraged us to invite the Holy Spirit to fill our lives. Broken before the Lord, I prayed in faith for the Spirit's anointing and immediately two words of an unknown language came into my mind. As I whispered these I thought, 'Oh no, not tongues!' In a panic, I said to God, 'Lord, I don't understand that,' and He replied, 'I know Paul, but I do.' Then the Holy Spirit reminded me of a day, many months previously, when He had spoken to me through Scripture in Song, 'Call unto me and I will answer you, and show you great and wondrous things which thou knowest not.' (Jeremiah 33:3 A.V.) At that time I had prayed, 'Lord that's for me – show me things I have never experienced before.' Now in the freezing tent, God was assuring me that He had heard and was answering my prayer. I rushed to tell Priscilla what had happened, and then sneaked off to be alone and prayed, 'God if that was you, do it again.' I learned another word of my prayer tongue, and from then it grew and became a fluent language. The same evening, at the main celebration, Ken McGreavy spoke on the subject of the Holy Spirit, and others from our Carryduff group responded. We were counselled by Floyd McClung, who gave us very practical advice on how to know the leading of the

Holy Spirit. I was beginning to learn that the Holy Spirit is not an uncontrollable force which invades our lives, but a person who gently and lovingly leads His children and speaks through them.

On the following day, I went with a friend, Tom McCann, to hear a strange figure dressed in black leather trousers and a black shirt, speaking on the subject of prophecy. His name was Gerald Coates, and he asked people in the audience who owned a copy of Darby's Synopsis of the Bible to raise their hands. Of course I had a copy. John Nelson Darby was the founder of the Brethren Movement, and this weighty volume took pride of place on my bookshelf. I stuck my hand in the air, and was promptly told to throw the book in the bin! Mr. Coates went on to tell the audience that those who had never heard of Darby had had a merciful release. I listened in amazement as he dismissed the dispensationalists, and asserted that Jesus gave the Holy Spirit to empower the Church and His gifts to equip the saints, then, now and until He returns! My Christian faith was a driving force in my life, and my relationship with the Lord had brought about many changes, but now there were stirrings at a deeper level in my being. For years I had given little conscious thought to my father's desertion of our family. I attended an all-night prayer meeting during which we were divided into small groups. The leader of the prayer session suggested that we spend some time praying for our parents. Suddenly I became aware of a mental block in my mind. How could I pray for a man who had hurt me so much? It had never honestly occurred to me that God could require such a thing. I had asked the Holy Spirit to invade my life with His power, and He was now demonstrating that power to heal. As I struggled to express a concern for my father in a prayer, God began to release some of the pain, which I could not have acknowledged, and He replaced it with a desire to allow Him to continue to touch this area of my life.

I returned home from Spring Harvest, excited about my new relationship with the Holy Spirit and all it could mean in my life and ministry. Not so my wife! Priscilla's family background was godly and stable, and she believed that God had brought us together so that she could keep me on the straight and narrow. She was really struggling now that I appeared to have gone completely off the road! For a while, we seemed to be going in totally different directions. Priscilla could not understand why I was insisting on a new experience with the Holy Spirit, when men like her father, 'a better Christian than you'll ever be,' managed without it. She heard me muttering one night and asked if I was praying in tongues. When I said, 'Yes,' she replied, 'Please don't do it in bed with me.' It was 1984 before Priscilla began to share my joy in the Holy Spirit. She went into hospital in January and, on her own birthday, gave birth to our third daughter, Susan. While in hospital, she read Appointment in Jerusalem by Lydia Prince, and the story stirred something in her spirit. A few weeks later, Tom McCann and I began a series of New Life in the Spirit seminars, which culminated in praying with a small group from the fellowship to be filled with the Holy Spirit. We laid hands on Priscilla, and God began to open her heart. Soon after that, while up in the night with the baby, she experienced a release in the Spirit and began to speak in a new prayer language.

In our Sunday morning meetings, I had tackled 1 Corinthians chapter twelve with renewed fervour. Some folk were open, others were not. I tried to be sensitive on the issue of the Holy Spirit, talking then in terms of a new experience of God. I was neither brave enough, nor clear enough in my mind, to openly teach the baptism in the Holy Spirit as a necessary experience subsequent to conversion, but then the women were still wearing head coverings, and I was to get used to doing U turns! As we began to acknowledge and expect the ministries of the Holy Spirit, our church meetings were electric! At first it was all me, visions, dreams, prophecies and messages in tongues. Then others began to speak out in faith, and we learned to minister to one another. All the time new folk were being drawn into fellowship with us.

One evening, a friend from the Crescent Church, Belfast, brought a young girl called Faye to us for help. I knew very little about the ministry of deliverance, but I could see that she was clearly suffering under the powers of Satan. We left her in the kitchen with one of the women, who tried to minister to her while the rest of us prayed in the other room. When I went in after some time to see how things were going, I discovered the two wrestling! Faye was contorting in snake-like movements and we were afraid. We managed to calm her and, after several visits, she seemed to have received some help. Eventually, however, after getting into trouble with the police and several suicide attempts, some years later Faye did take her own life. It was a sad introduction to the realm of demonic strongholds in people's lives.

I realized that I lacked both knowledge and experience in this area. I began to study the subject of deliverance and read Deliver us from Evil, by Don Basham. Shortly after, I received a phone call from a man, whom I had known several years before. He asked to meet me urgently, and when I picked him up he was in a most dishevelled state. He told me that he was separated from his wife, so I offered to take him home and talk to both of them. As we drove past a particular road, suddenly he threw a fit in the car, shaking and convulsing horribly. I pulled over and, when he recovered, he admitted that he was living with two primary school teachers, who were practising witches. The seizure had come on him as we had passed by where they lived! We proceeded to his home but his wife was out, so I collected Tom McCann and went to Clifford Edgar's house. We offered to pray with the man, but as we reached out our hands to minister, he reacted violently. It took all three of us to hold him down, as we cried out to the Lord for deliverance from the demons so clearly present. That night he made a profession of faith and experienced a dramatic healing and cleansing. We helped him financially so that he might escape imprisonment, and he remained a member of our church for some time.

Ministering in the power of the Holy Spirit was going to mean getting my hands dirty, but God was at work among us in a wonderful way and we were learning all the time.

At my invitation, Pastor Wally North came to speak at our meeting and there followed accusations that I was turning the fellowship into a Pentecostal church. Several people left and serious cracks were beginning to develop. God spoke clearly to me from the story of the young centurion in Luke chapter seven. He was able to command obedience from his soldiers because he was also a man under authority. I was beginning to sense the need for personal support as I struggled to keep things together.

I discovered that change was here to stay as we were forced to address one issue after another. As the church had grown, infants, including our own three daughters, had spilled over into the next room. It was proposed that we should tape the sermons for those supervising the children, and I heard of someone in Belfast who might reproduce these. It was thus that I began regular visits to the Belmont Road office of Christian Audio Tapes, run by Milford Craig. In the same building were housed the offices of Down Christian Trust (D.C.T.), the Holywood off-shoot from Bangor Christian Trust. During a visit to the Belmont Road, I was introduced to Peter Yarr, one of the leaders in the Trust. He was warm and encouraging, interested in my life and ministry. We built up a friendship over the months, and eventually I shared with him my desire to be linked in with another fellowship, so that I could receive input into my own life.

Peter introduced me to the concept of personal pastoral care or Shepherding, and arranged a meeting with Hugh Jervis, another leader in the Trust. Hugh agreed to be my 'shepherd,' and met with me every Friday morning for a year. I praise God for Hugh and Aileen Jervis, a special couple who became great friends. Hugh is a gentle, quiet man who wisely guided me into a place where I heard from God on every issue in my life. Although I always had plenty of money, I was not a good manager of my finances. Hugh patiently helped me to bring this area under God's control. Also through his ministry, Priscilla and I were both set free from her desire to keep me 'right,' and we began to enjoy the leading of the Holy Spirit in our marriage.

Although we were personally benefiting from the relationship with members of D.C.T., the rumblings continued in our own fellowship. I invited Hugh and Peter to speak, and there were those who resented their involvement. We were immersing ourselves in the teachings of Derek Prince, and central was the practice of Shepherding. I was submitting my life to Hugh's guidance, and was tithing directly to him. Some in our own group wanted to submit to me in the same way, and I received several personal tithes. Although I had wanted more authority, it rested uneasily with me. I was uncomfortable with making decisions concerning other people's lives, so in my desire to help them I tried to encourage those in our fellowship to hear from God for themselves. I held a strong influence over individuals, however, and it was not always for good.

The issue of Shepherding, along with differing interpretations of the baptism in the Holy Spirit, finally led to a split in our Carryduff church. One third of the fellowship said that they were with us, the others said 'no.' We were heartbroken. These were people we loved and with whom we had shared so much. Retrospect is a humbling thing and I can now see how destructive my arrogance was. I handled the situation badly and immaturely, believing that we had discovered the truth, and that those who did not agree deserved to be left behind as we steamrolled our way forward. My gentle wife, who was more aware than I of my character weaknesses, suffered terribly.

The fellowship continued for some time with only eleven members. God was gracious to us in spite of our faults and others joined us, among them George and Alice Graham. I visited these old friends one day to share what God was doing in our lives and discovered Alice hungry for someone to lead her to receive the baptism in the Holy Spirit. She and George started to attend our meeting and grow in the Lord, but when she became pregnant, there was great concern for her health. In a previous pregnancy with her twins, she had been extremely ill, and this time again she was so sick that the baby and her own life were in danger. In the fellowship we fasted and prayed in faith that God would heal her. The sickness stopped, and in due course baby Roy was born safely.

It was our first experience of supernatural healing, and we were eager to know more.

As a group we attended a week of prayer and fasting organized by the Bangor Christian Trust. This was supported by four Methodist ministers, and we became aware that John Kelly's prayer was to see renewal within the Methodist Church. We were welcomed warmly, but left feeling confused. I knew that God had brought us to these people living in community in Bangor and Holywood because of relationship, but I did not share their vision for Methodism. In the summer of 1984 this question was resolved when the Methodist Church in effect asked the special fellowships to leave, and they became churches in their own right. In Bangor, King's Fellowship was formed, and in Holywood a decision was made to move further into East Belfast, and Down Christian Trust became Christian Fellowship Church (C.F.C.).

We continued to enjoy fellowship with the folk in Carryduff, and some of our new acquaintances observed that our love for one another was stronger than that between people who made a lot of noise about the uniqueness of their covenant relationships. I was feeling more and more frustrated, however, as Priscilla and I continued to form strong friendships with folks in the city, and we felt drawn towards the Belfast church.

That year we went along to a summer camp in Castlewellan, run by some people from C.F.C. There we witnessed a deliverance ministry which left us feeling terrified. The practice then seemed to be to call everything a demon, unless it proved otherwise. I now recognize that the events there were somewhat bizarre and excessive, and regret that the camp left several casualties, but we were the newcomers and thought this was all normal. However, the overall effect on our lives was to bring us from A to Z in terms of spiritual gifts, in a short space of time.

Firmly rooted in the Brethren tradition and imbued with an enduring passion for the recovery of New Testament realities, I found myself being drawn into this new way of being church and its emphasis on the supernatural. I had begun to taste new wine and was thirsty for more. Furthermore I had an allegiance to Hugh, my 'shepherd,' and a genuine affection for our Belfast friends. I was becoming increasingly convinced that I needed to be in a place where I could learn from others, and enjoy the protection of their authority. I was being heavily influenced at that time, while still believing myself to be an independent thinker. The bit was firmly between my teeth! A decision regarding the future of the Carryduff group had to be made. We had our own week of prayer and fasting, and then agreed that God was leading us to throw our lot in with Christian Fellowship Church. It was January 1985, and we were excited as we set our sights on Belfast. It was only a half hour's drive on a Sunday morning to meet with them in Avoniel Leisure Centre. We became the Carryduff homegroup, and I remained their leader. I missed the preaching, but I was very hopeful about the future.

4

Are you Charismatic?

The previous two decades had been a time of charismatic renewal in Ireland. The Pentecostal Movement had come to the fore with its emphasis on the person of the Holy Spirit, but the civil unrest which surfaced in the late sixties, caused Christians to cry out to God for an expression of church which would help to heal division.

A significant figure in the movement of the Holy Spirit throughout Ireland during that time, was Keith Gerner. An 'Oxbridge' man educated in the classics, he came to teach in Portora Royal School, Enniskillen. After his baptism in the Holy Spirit, Keith was involved in the rise of the Pentecostal Movement in the mid sixties. His subsequent association with Roman Catholics on the charismatic scene led to him being ostracized by the Pentecostals, and he embarked on an independent evangelistic and teaching ministry.

He established the Cherith Trust in Holywood, Co.Down from which base he distributed books and tapes and travelled throughout Ireland. There are many individuals and small pockets of believers all over the South, who trace their conversion and baptism in the Holy Spirit to this man's ministry. Keith still lives in Northern Ireland, although he spends much of his time abroad. I believe that the Church in Ireland owes him a great debt, the extent of which only history will reveal.

Locally, the beginning of charismatic renewal resulted from prayer meetings which sprang up in response to the start of the present 'Troubles.' In the late sixties and early seventies, when the civil rights debate was at its height, Queen's University, Belfast, a hotbed of unrest, also became the centre of student prayer for the province. A group of young men and women, fearing civil war, as violence accompanied the movement for equality and justice, met to cry out to God for His intervention. Among these students was John Kelly, who even after he completed his medical training, continued to meet with others, including Peter Yarr. They joined together every evening and all day Saturday for intercession.

Around the same time a charismatic fellowship began to meet in the Y.M.C.A. building in Howard Street, Belfast. This was led by Tom Smail and David Bailie. The fellowship broke new ground because it was interdenominational, and encouraged people to be open to a movement of the Holy Spirit. God was also at work in a new way in the Church of Ireland Centre at Queen's. A group of visiting Americans caused a stir by praying with students to be baptized in the Holy Spirit. Rev. Cecil Kerr was in charge of the centre, and for him the early seventies were years of personal renewal. He visited the States and, on his return, began to hold early morning communion services twice a week. These were attended by those meeting to pray for Ireland, and the streams of renewal in Northern Ireland were beginning to flow together. Cecil Kerr held a regular charismatic midweek meeting in Belfast until his move to Rostrevor in South Down. There he established a Renewal Centre, now known throughout the world for its efforts to bring together Roman Catholics and Protestants in the name of Jesus, and provide the opportunity for spiritual refreshment to those, from every denomination, seeking to promote unity in a divided country.

As the movement for renewal became associated with reconciliation, the stream broadened out. A National Service Committee for Charismatic Renewal was established, which incorporated both Roman Catholics and Protestants. Attempting to co-operate at this level proved too ambitious, however, and this committee was disbanded. Separate service committees responsible for arranging conferences and promoting spiritual renewal, were formed north and south. The movement for renewal was beginning to diversify.

The Northern Service Committee included Cecil Kerr, John Kelly and Peter Yarr. John and Peter were by then based in Bangor, North Down, where the initial emphasis was on interdenominational activity, such as Scripture Union camps and Crusaders groups. They were experiencing an outpouring of the Holy Spirit and wanted to give expression to this renewal. By 1975/76 the main thrust had changed from intercession to community, and Bangor Christian Trust was formed. The Trust's home was within the Methodist Church until such time as the traditional denomination could no longer contain an interdenominational group with an emphasis on the Holy Spirit and Shepherding. Also in North Down, Rev.David Bailie had established a charismatic witness within the Presbyterian Church.

In the south of Ireland, Eustace Street, Dublin was the venue for a prayer meeting in the early seventies. Roman Catholics were getting involved in spiritual renewal. A leadership emerged which fed into the National Service Committee. Eventually the Light of Christ Community was formed in Dublin. This and the Lamb of God Community in Belfast were almost totally Catholic. Although interdenominational in purpose, Bangor Christian Trust and the Community of the King, which had emerged from Gilnahirk Presbyterian Church, were predominantly Protestant.

After the collapse of the National Service Committee, nothing happened on a national scale for a number of years, apart from occasional Pentecost rallies and a Charismatic Leaders' Conference in 1984. In the ecumenical stream, there were attempts to form united new churches, and the Community of the King tried to merge with Belfast Christian Family, but these were dogged by disagreements. In the South, the early communities have emerged as New Churches. The Charismatic Movement has continued, but without a flagship.

This decade has seen a dramatic growth in New Churches. Some of these could still be called house churches, others have outgrown private homes, but meet in public buildings. Not all are averse to owning property, but while they may meet in a church building, they retain elements which distinguish them from traditional denominations. These include the absence of ordained clergy and an emphasis on the priesthood of all believers. The practice of Body ministry involves the exercise of the gifts of the Holy Spirit.

Christian Fellowship Church was one such New Church. In joining I was beginning to flow in a charismatic stream. God is more interested in lives than labels, however, and he was about to challenge mine again. We had made our move on the basis of relationship, but were about to discover that 'new' did not mean that there was no room for fundamental change.

5

Resigned to Serve

Becoming part of the Christian Fellowship Church family, was a culture shock. The large leisure centre in the heart of East Belfast was a far cry from rural Carryduff. We had come from the familiarity and comfort of a house church, albeit a disintegrating one, and we were soon to discover that there was no security in numbers. C.F.C. had its own problems. We were immediately aware of the tensions, firstly between Belfast and the sister church in Bangor, and among the local elders, who were struggling with their roles in a new church situation.

Once we were 'in,' we began to understand the full significance of the Shepherding Movement, and its implications for church life. This movement, which had dominated the life of the Bangor Christian Trust, first emerged in the U.S.A., during the time of charismatic renewal in the late sixties and early seventies. Four well-known Christian leaders from divergent ministries came together; Derek Prince, originally from England, Charles Simpson, Bob Mumford and Ern Baxter. These were later joined by Don Basham and became known as the Fort Lauderdale Five. After hearing a fellow leader confess to sexual sin, they became very concerned about the lack of pastoral care in most churches. Recognizing their personal need for support, they began to pastor one another and 'cover' each other's ministry. Thus was born the Discipleship Movement, which grew dramatically on the strength of its authors' reputations.

It resulted almost immediately in deep divisions in the churches in America, because of the authoritarian emphasis of instructions on accountability. Books were being written on the subject of Shepherding, as this form of discipling became known. Derek Prince put together the bones of this teaching, and Charles Simpson added the flesh. In reacting to the lack of pastoral care, they went to opposite extremes.

Shepherding stressed the need for every believer to be in a relationship of submission on a one-to-one basis. In practice this led to a patriarchal pyramid in which all male members were 'covered' by an authority within the church or fellowship group. It followed that wives were 'covered' by their husbands. For those who embraced Shepherding, pastoral care became the dominant ministry, and an imbalance resulted. Men gifted in prophecy and evangelism were appointed as pastors, and those ministries were being lost to the Church. The saying goes, 'Five minutes with a prophet, six months with a pastor.' Prophets do not often make good pastors, and many people's lives were being damaged by 'shepherds' who were out of their gifting.

In Ireland, John Kelly and Peter Yarr were inspired by the teachings of Derek Prince on tape. They made contact with him during a visit to England, and he put them in touch with another member of the Shepherding Movement, Eric Krieger, who became their 'shepherd.' He in turn was 'shepherded' by Charles Simpson, a foundation stone of the movement.

During the years that followed, many of the practices of the Shepherding Movement were at their most extreme in Northern Ireland. Groups in Bangor, Holywood and Belfast were worst affected, but its influence spread throughout the province. The manipulation and control of young people gave rise to public concern, and provided controversial subject matter for a television documentary. It was taught that an individual had no right of perspective on his 'shepherd,' to whom he was committed in covenant relationship. The one in authority was believed to have the big picture, and he was to be honoured and obeyed. Everyone was allocated a personal 'shepherd,' and each leader had several people in his care.

The extent to which control was exercised over an individual, depended largely on the personality and maturity of the 'shepherd.' Many strong directions were given in matters ranging from dress to marriage partners. Young people, determined to see the kingdom of God established, moved house, changed their lifestyle, laid down their lives sacrificially and, in some cases, surrendered the right to a university education.

In C.F.C., many of these practices went unquestioned for years. I myself was only made aware of the dangers when I began to realize the effects on individuals, who were being robbed of a personal walk with God, in exchange for dependence on others. By the time I came into contact with the movement, through my relationship with Peter and Hugh, there were already major disagreements among the hierarchy. The ideal of covenant relationship was being held up, while those purporting to espouse it were openly criticizing each other. When I was in leadership in the church, I personally witnessed bitter animosity between the founders of the Shepherding Movement.

Even as a newcomer, I was aware of the rumblings of discontent. The elders were struggling. Their acceptance of the teachings on Shepherding was not producing 'koinonia' fellowship. There was a widening gap between theory and practice, which led to deep suspicions and mistrust. Overall there was a lack of communication, and a growing resistance to the inflexible regime imposed through Shepherding. Individuals were suffering, but felt unable to express their grievances. There was no room for discussion.

I had understood Shepherding in terms of pastoral care, but I soon became aware of the strong element of control. The women in the fellowship had endured harsh treatment at the hands of men, who saw their only role as caring for children and making themselves beautiful for their husbands.

The eldership at that time comprised Hugh Jervis, John Thompson and Peter Yarr, with Peter as the leading elder. Peter was a businessman with a penchant for forming new companies. He did not enjoy the additional demands of church life, such as conducting weddings, but he did have a vision for a permanent home for C.F.C. As a homegroup leader, I was included on a committee formed to address this issue. When the Church of God building at Strandtown on the Holywood Road came on the market, Peter put together an amazing purchasing plan. In order to buy it, we had to take out a loan of 350 thousand pounds, and another 80 thousand pounds was to be borrowed on our behalf by the Church of God. We were to service these and borrow further sums from a church in York, and our own members, in total, 520 thousand pounds! This scheme was foolishness in human terms, but I believe that in the midst of confusion, Peter heard from God, and we gave him our support. A system for repayment depended on the generous pledges of members, and by the grace of God the monthly demands were met. In September 1985 we began to use the Strandtown building for our meeting on Sunday afternoons, and took final possession on January 1st 1986. As I look back on what happened then, I am amazed that, although we were soon to come under God's judgement in respect of serious error, in His purpose and plan He provided a wonderful facility for us that has proved to be a great blessing.

Meanwhile the grumblings continued. During the summer of 1985, I was ill for a while. I believed that God had 'grounded' me so that I could have time to reflect. Hugh came to visit, and I began to share some of my concerns with him. Hugh was still shepherding me, and we had a good relationship. To my surprise, on this occasion, he admitted to personal struggles. His words were, 'I feel like I'm jogging in a suit of armour.' I decided to go to the elders and offer some constructive criticism. As a result they called my bluff and ordained me an elder. Totally convinced that God was working in C.F.C., I took this new responsibility very seriously and became a part-time worker in the church. All my business was conducted between Tuesday and Thursday, and I devoted the remainder of my time to pastoral care. New people were joining the church, and Priscilla and I ran a foundation course. I also took charge of the youth work, and from time to time was even known to lead the worship. My Brethren training in unaccompanied singing came in useful! As regards responsibility, I continued to 'shepherd' some men from the Carryduff group, but felt that as an elder I had moved to the government benches, while many of my friends remained in opposition. There were rumblings in middle management, with accusations of 'bad leadership,' while we responded by blaming 'bad attitudes.' I began to find myself the target for discontented people, and I discovered the isolation of leadership. Why had we ever left the comparative peace and security of Carryduff? None-the-less I was there by conviction, and prepared to weather the storm. I was buoyed up by a firm belief that God was working out His purposes in my life, through all circumstances. God saw my struggle, and spoke very clearly to me personally. I could not fully comprehend much of what He said at the time, but in hindsight I could see the Holy Spirit at work in the preparation of my heart.

On one occasion, while a friend was praying with me, I had a vision in the Spirit. I was sitting in a darkened room. The door was flung open, and I became aware of the presence of a man. Although I did not see His face, I knew that it was the Lord. He ushered me into a room filled with an overwhelming, brilliant light. Its beauty was astounding. Jesus then opened yet another door and outside was darkness. His word to me was, 'Now you bring others into the light.' I wondered if God was calling me to be an evangelist, but Dr. Ronnie Alcorn, friend and trustee of the church, suggested that God had sent me to help those involved in the Fellowship Movement to come out of darkness into light. This seemed too fantastic, so I filed it under 'pending.' Early in that same year, I had another supernatural experience. Along with two friends from my homegroup, I went to hear the late Sandy Thompson in Lisburn. Sandy had a dynamic prophetic ministry. There was a crowd at the meeting, so we were not able to sit together. Sandy emerged from the prayer room and began to read from the Bible. Almost immediately he paused, looked into the congregation and pointed to me. He identified my two friends sitting elsewhere, and said that he knew that I was their 'shepherd.' He described me as a 'giant,' and when he asked me to stand up he joked, 'You are a giant!' He spoke with accuracy about our group meeting in Carryduff, and mentioned an older man who had ploughed the ground for me. I believe that this referred to Jim Scott, my father-in-law. Sandy told me that although this man would continue to pray for me, I was not to go back to where he was, but forward into new things. Someday, he prophesied, there would be a call, and I would be required to stand in the gap. He encouraged me to stir up the gifts of pastor and teacher, and to dig deep into God's Word. In the light of the events that followed, I believe that this was a foreshadowing of things to come. I was grateful for encouragements received through God's prophets.

God was at work in my life and I became aware of unfinished business in relation to my father. Jamie Buckingham visited the church in May 1986 and spoke on the subject of forgiveness. That night God touched me again and I realized that, although I had begun to pray for my father, I still felt a deep sense of resentment towards him. A father's rejection of a child is impossible for many to understand. The effect on the child and its implications for the remainder of his life, are an even greater mystery. Why should the dramatic scenes from childhood still hold the power to reduce a grown man to tears? When Jamie made an appeal, I was the first to respond. He prayed with me as I expressed to God my willingness to forgive my father. I could never excuse what he had done, but God's love released the grace to forgive on the same basis as His forgiveness, the death and resurrection of Jesus Christ. Another layer of the onion was peeled off, and I felt free to consider making contact with my father.

When God's blessing is on a group of people, mistakes are covered by love. If, however, God has withdrawn His hand of blessing, neither slick presentation nor great schemes and structures, can hide the fact. Acutely aware of the problems in C.F.C., the elders disbanded and re-formed homegroups, and we dissected Peter Yarr's sermons on a weekly basis, all in an attempt to evade the issue of the absence of God's anointing on us. We were learning a very important lesson. We thought that God had blessed us because of Shepherding, but we began to realize that He had blessed us in spite of it. Dick Iverson once said, 'Be careful what you build when the tide of God's Spirit is in and on you, for when the tide goes out you can see the debris of what you have built.' In other words, God's blessing and anointing cover human foul-ups, but watch it when the Spirit moves on! We heard that John Wimber was coming to London in Spring 1986, so we decided to go and talk to him. Perhaps he could give us the recipe for success in church life? His wise reply was, 'I'm not selling anything, it's the Holy Spirit.' About seventy of us had come to the conference, and many were blessed. Further conferences were already planned for Ireland during the summer.

After our return, the elders had lunch with Charles Slagle, on tour from Arizona, U.S.A. with his prophetic presentation in song. As we were leaving, Charles spoke a word of prophecy from the Lord, 'I see you in a ruined building surrounded by rubble; but don't worry, I'm in control!' John Thompson and I were due to leave the next day for a holiday in Portugal with our wives, and we joked about our apartment, 'Perhaps it's not finished.' But God was again preparing me for more serious devastation in the lives of His children. Our holiday with John and Linda went ahead in July, and was for us all a special time when we began to share our lives as never before. Together we faced the reality that things were not as they should have been, personally or corporately. We were open and honest with each other and returned home with a new perspective, eager for God to redeem the situation.

John Wimber arrived in August as arranged. He held conferences in Dublin and Belfast, and members of the Wimber team took a series of meetings in C.F.C. We watched in amazement as grown men wept before the Lord; but our hearts were hard and we called them 'wimps.' After all, we were shown films like Rocky 1 and 2 on the men's week-end, in order to teach us durability and instil the manly virtues of endurance and perseverance! But God's Holy Spirit was melting hearts, that He might bring us to repentance.

Both Peter Yarr and I had supernatural experiences of God during the time of the Wimber conferences.

The crisis in the church, and in our own lives, was coming to a head, and we were aware that something drastic was about to happen.

An influential book at that time was The Transformation of the Inner Man, by John and Paula Sanford. It contained an expose of the Shepherding Movement and its idolatrous practices. John Thompson was convicted through reading it, and his willingness to hear God's voice brought us all to a crossroads.

On an unforgettable Friday morning at the end of August 1986, the four elders and our wives met together. John Thompson announced that he felt he could no longer continue as an elder, and said that he believed God was asking us as leaders to repent. The rest of us found an echo in our hearts, as John voiced concern for the lack of direction and anointing in our church life. We met again in the evening and agreed that we could not continue simply making adjustments, radical change was needed. It was time to lay the leadership down and come before God in repentance. We decided to hand the church over to the people and hope that they would hear from God, as each of us sought personal guidance.

In the days that followed, there was much heart searching and anguish. I cried out to God to reveal to me what He was saying in the situation. On the Sunday morning, I found myself standing in front of the congregation sharing what God had put on my heart. I had been challenged by the account of Abraham's burial of Sarah in Genesis chapter twenty-three. God revealed that in burying Sarah, Abraham was burying God's former channel of blessing. Isaac, the child of the covenant, had been born to him by Sarah. He did not know that round the corner there was a new wife, Keturah, and more sons.

Abraham was also burying the sense of his greatest failure. Twice he had lied about Sarah in order to save his own skin. As he laid his wife to rest, he must have been conscious of his sin against her and God. Lastly, Abraham was burying the love of his life. Abraham mourned and wept over Sarah and was finally buried with her. Like Abraham, I was feeling a great sense of loss. God had blessed me and I loved the ministry in the church, but now He was asking me to lay down all that I held dear. The sense of failure was very painful because yet again I had blown it as a leader. Nevertheless I loved God and His work, and was dedicated to seeing His kingdom extended. How could I let go of all that? God's word to me was, 'bury your dead,' the former channel of blessing, my failure and the greatest love of my life.

A special meeting was announced to take place the following Tuesday. There each elder made a short speech, and we formally resigned as leaders of the church. We cited three reasons for our resignations:
1. Self-righteousness. We believed that we were better than other churches and fellowships.
2. Manipulation. Lives had been controlled through Shepherding.
3. Idolatry. We had given to men the honour due to God alone.

It was a very emotional and dramatic occasion. Leaders and people alike shed tears; some spoke of mourning for mistakes, and burying things once cherished. Overall there was a tremendous sense of God's grace, as rejoicing in His mercy mingled with the tears. The essential element was a willingness to let go of the past, and look to the Holy Spirit to lead us on level ground (Psalm 143:10). A word of warning came from the book of Jonah, '... those who cling to worthless idols, forfeit the grace that could be theirs.' (Jonah 2:8) Some church leaders were horrified by what we had done; others were able to see the hand of God at work. Cecil Kerr, from the Renewal Centre in Rostrevor, phoned and said, 'You'll be the laughing stock of Northern Ireland, but isn't it fantastic! Repentance is what is needed in the Church today.' God had brought us to breaking point, and no-one could see the path ahead. Priscilla and I wept before the Lord as He dealt with our personal failings. In the turmoil, we questioned why God had led us into a situation on which He had His hand in judgement. As relative new-comers we were not tainted with some of the excesses of the past, but when God began to reveal our hearts to us, we took our share of the blame. I recall a day when driving home, I felt the weight of my own sin so heavy. I went straight to my room and flung myself on the bed, weeping. As I prayed, the Holy Spirit showed me the extent of my hardness of attitude. He said, 'Paul, you are harder on other people than I am, and you are harder on yourself than I am.' 'Lord, that's impossible,' I argued, 'because

Your way is perfect and all men have sinned and come short of your glory.' He replied, 'I am God, and my dealings with man are in love and through the blood of Jesus. Yours are based on your hurt and your hardness of heart.' He went on to reveal to me that the origin of this was in my relationship with my father. He had totally failed me and the child in me was angry. This root of bitterness led to my subsequent rejection of anyone who did not live up to my expectations. From then I learned to withdraw my love from those who disagreed with me. I had begun to acknowledge how my own life had been scarred by my father's behaviour, but I had not been fully aware that my attitude towards others had also been adversely affected. Now it was time to take personal responsibility.

God took me back to 1984, to the folks in Carryduff who had left the fellowship. He showed me that my strong determination to follow my convictions had resulted in people being mistreated and hurt. Over the next few weeks, I visited those people, personally repented and made my peace with them. It was a powerful time in my life, a painful but valuable cleansing and healing process. I understood the grace of God as never before, that my rebellious, sinful ways past, present and future were forgiven through the death of Jesus. I was assured of God's mercy, but at that time I thought He could never use me again. I believed that my ministry was over, but it was enough to know that Father loved me.

I returned to my business full-time, while Peter and

Hugh remained in the employ of the church. The elders had made a united stand, but it took several meetings before we were sure that there were no hidden agendas. It was particularly difficult for Peter Yarr as the father and leader of the church to lay it down. The other trustees of the church, Les McKeown, Stuart Graham and Ronnie Alcorn handled the immediate crisis. They called three days of prayer and fasting, after which a vote was taken for an interim leadership. The former elders decided not to serve on this team. We were all waiting for guidance regarding our futures in leadership. After a few short weeks, however, the interim leaders asked me if I would do the preaching on Sundays, without privilege.

I agreed to this on the strength of words of encouragement given to me by two church members. At my lowest point, Jennifer Gough, now my secretary, gave me a promise from Acts 18:9, 'Do not be afraid; keep on speaking, do not be silent... because I have many people in this city.' Another person shared that the preaching of God's Word was the only thing which was going to unite people in the aftermath of the resignations. In the midst of devastation, therefore, I embarked on a series on the life of David in the wilderness. There was a sense of brokenness in the meetings. Things were changing as the Holy Spirit anointed the preaching and was again released among us. As I trekked through my own wilderness, the grace of God became my favourite theme.

Shortly after the resignations, Roger Forster, Graham Kendrick and Ken McGreavy arrived for a pre-booked weekend, a joint venture with two other fellowships. They walked into chaos. At one meeting Ken called me up to pray with people, and I can still feel the pain of failure which made me most reluctant to get involved. I sat in the meetings aching. From my youth I had wanted to serve the Lord. Was it all over now? Roger Forster spoke on Elijah and Elisha and recounted the story of Elisha's call. Elijah came to him as he was ploughing in the field, but when the prophet threw his cloak around him, Elisha took his yoke of oxen and slaughtered them. He also burned the ploughing equipment and cooked the meat as a sacrifice before he set out to follow Elijah. (1 Kings 19) That night, I too heard God's call. In an unmistakable voice, He assured me of His love, His forgiveness and His continued desire to use me in the building of His kingdom. Furthermore He told me that in six months from then, I would be leaving behind my business and serving Him full-time. Moreover I was to ask Peter Yarr for his mantle. Despair was giving way to hope, and as a seal on the birth of something new, we made the happy discovery that God was blessing us with a fourth child.

Around that time a local church leader, David Matthews, returned from England and was both a stabilizing influence and a personal encouragement. I continued to preach on Sundays, and waited for God's time. The interim leadership team was struggling in limbo, unsure of the extent of its authority. Confined to bed as a result of a back injury, I heard from God again, 'Do not touch my appointed leadership; do not take on any responsibility in the church until Peter lays it down.' Peter returned from a conference the next day and came to talk about how God was directing him. He said that He had been clearly told to finally leave the leadership of C.F.C. and hand the church over to me. I shared what God had spoken to me, and asked him for his mantle. I don't know which of us was more astonished at God's timing and confirmation of His purposes.

Peter told the interim leaders that he was leaving, and it was agreed that as the founder of the church, he should set in place a new group of elders. He chose ten men, the three of us who had already served, along with George Dines, Ian Mitchell, Alan George, Ian Barr, Stuart Graham, Jim Quinn and Stephen Cummings. I became the chairman of this somewhat unwieldy team. We were ten individuals, afraid of authority yet jockeying for position. We discussed things like what colour scheme to use in the church, but there was no clear word of direction. In hindsight, I think we had thrown the baby out with the bathwater, and a sense of God's anointing on leadership was missing.

In the meantime, Peter Yarr was looking for personal guidance. Still in the pay of the church, he and Sharon rented out their house and took their sons to America to spend six months with John Wimber. On the Sunday before he left, he laid hands on me and formally handed over the leadership. Although Peter was to return to Ireland, take a job and eventually attend C.F.C. again, for this time the mantle was mine.

These events marked a significant turning point in the life of the church. God was working out his purposes as revealed prophetically months and years before. On April 1st 1986, I left my business and became full-time in C.F.C., six months after the time when I heard God's call. There were no funds in the church coffers, but a substantial gift released money for the first month's salary, and from then we prayed it in.

Much of my work in the weeks that followed, was pastoral. The Shepherding Movement had left many casualties. Young people had laid down their lives to feed men's pride, and the resulting resentments and grief were deep-seated. It was a chapter in our lives that we wanted to close. For some people however, it was a long, slow process of recovery as they learned how to take responsibility for their own lives before God. The Holy Spirit ministered inner healing to many, but there are still some walking wounded around today.

6

Finding a Vision

A key element in our resignations as elders, was a conscious handing over of the church to the Lord. Although some of us were back in harness, His was the voice we wanted to hear. The team of ten struggled on for a few weeks without any real sense of direction. Agreements were bartered, but no-one felt free to take initiative. Finally, one elder identified the problem as a failure to acknowledge the one whom God had called into leadership in C.F.C. There followed a recognition of the authority given to me by God, and I was released to share the things He was revealing to my spirit.

We were a church of about 150 people, rattling around in a huge building, situated between working class East Belfast and the quiet suburb of Holywood. God began to give me a fresh vision of His plan to use ordinary, broken people in the extension of His kingdom. I saw the building at Strandtown filled to overflowing and set before the congregation a five-year plan, outlining the direction in which I believed God was taking us, including growth in attendance to one thousand.

1987 was a busy year for us. I started in my new job in C.F.C. on 1st April, we moved house from Carryduff into Belfast in May and our fourth daughter, Amy, was born in June. Our new home was only a few streets away from the Strandtown building. We had first viewed the property in January and our offer on it was accepted. We were unable to sell our house in Carryduff, however, but were so convinced that 21 Edgcumbe Gardens was God's choice for us, that we financed two mortgages for four months. We settled quickly in the area and God began to bless our family and church life. Week by week new people were joining in fellowship with us, and I experienced a fresh anointing in my teaching ministry. The preaching of the Word remained a vital ingredient in the on-going healing process for those damaged by the Shepherding Movement. God's truth proclaimed Sunday after Sunday in systematic Bible study, sought to address the errors of the past and lay a sure foundation for the future.

As we emerged from a dark period, we needed to sound a new note of celebration in our worship. Priscilla and I attended the wedding of Jim and Kitty Thompson. A young man sang, 'Oh, behold the Lamb...' The song was his own, and I recognized in him a special gift. Robin Mark became the worship leader in C.F.C. and had a significant input in taking the church forward. His sensitivity to the Holy Spirit, both in leading praise and in song-writing, served others in their search for inner healing and intimacy with God. Moreover, his songs with their Celtic flavour are an important ingredient in providing a cross-cultural link in Ireland.

The following months involved a process of unlearning, and developing new ways of relating to each other. Many were beginning to hear from God for themselves, after years of close shepherding. We were rediscovering the grace of God and enjoying His blessing upon us. It was a time of tremendous growth. We started a youth programme, a government training scheme, weekly house groups and summer camps. October 1988 saw the first Sunday Night at C.F.C., a time of praise and ministry, which is still very popular with visitors from other churches. We reached our target of one thousand attending within three years, and began to hold two services on a Sunday morning in order to accomodate the numbers.

By this time, we had revised the leadership team. Jim Thompson had been ordained an elder, four of the other elders had resigned, in order to concentrate on family and business life, and Peter Dornan had become our full-time youth leader. George Dines and Ian Mitchell had both moved out of Strandtown, with a view to planting sister churches in Holywood and Banbridge. At that stage we saw this as something these individuals had been called to do, not as an overall vision. The main focus was on building up the work in Strandtown, and my attitude to the church plant was, 'God bless her and all who sail in her.' Imagine an oil tanker hurtling along in one direction and then suddenly applying the brakes. It will still continue forward for a considerable distance, before it stops and turns. After our renunciation of the Shepherding Movement, the momentum of church continued for some months without a definite change of direction. We knew what we were not, but did not have a clear idea about what we were. Unconsciously, we were looking for an identity.

I received an invitation to a conference in England with the unlikely title, Apostles and Prophets for the Harvest. The list of sponsors was a Who's Who of the New Church movement: John Noble, Barney Coombes, Gerald Coates, Roger Forster and Terry Virgo. On the application form I was asked, 'To which of the above are you related?' I wrote, 'None,' and returned the form. A perplexed secretary phoned a few days later, insisting that I must be connected to one of the main groups, otherwise I should not have received an invitation. She inquired again, 'What stream are you in?' to which I replied, 'the Lagan!' Already in 1989, we in Ireland were being influenced by the New Churches in England. A welcome import was March for Jesus. In May of that year the March for Jesus committee hired the C.F.C. building for a pre-march rally, to be addressed by Gerald Coates. Along with other house church leaders, I was invited to meet him in the home of Robert Mearns (Laos Fellowship). Gerald was in fine form, holding forth about his favourite film, Ammadeus. I interjected facetiously that my favourite was, Seven Brides for Seven Brothers, but Gerald was not to be toppled from his soap box. No sense of humour, the English! I had not seen Gerald since the time of my baptism in the Holy Spirit at Spring Harvest, 1983. At the rally in our church, he spoke on the vision for March for Jesus, in the context of spiritual warfare. Suddenly he interrupted his talk and picked me out of the crowd. He then proceeded to deliver a detailed word of prophecy. He described me as a Christian statesman and bridge-builder, and said that I was going to have important relationships with three other people. This later became significant when George Hilary, Derek Poole, Andy McCaroll and I were involved in the early planning stages of Together for the Kingdom.

This word encouraged and excited me. Gerald seemed to be personally interested in what God was doing among us in C.F.C. A relationship between us and the Pioneer team started to develop. We began to see training opportunities for our young people and we sent some to join Training in Evangelism (T.I.E.) teams in England. A group of us also went to a Pioneer conference in Guilford, where the speaker was Dudley Daniels. We thoroughly enjoyed it and in return invited Greald to speak at a Sunday night meeting in December. This was a great success, so we followed it up with a Way Forward week-end.

At this time the elders in C.F.C. were giving serious consideration to the possibility of being linked in to Pioneer Ministries. We were aware of the benefits of relationship with other movements through which we could receive help and support, but were reluctant to repeat the mistakes of the past. Our week-end was to be a time of hearing from God for clear direction. I spoke on the Friday night and my conclusion was that as a church we still lacked an identiy. Did we need to look for help, input, covering? Perhaps Gerald had the answer? He was keen for us to forge stronger links with them, but we knew that we had to hear from God. In February 1990, Peter Dornan and I went to a Key Leaders' conference. I personally benefited from the ministry of the Holy Spirit at that conference. Johnny Barr, an Elim pastor with a prophetic ministry, prayed with me specifically about satanic holds in my life coming through previous generations.

In the summer of 1990, Steve Clifford (chairman of March for Jesus) was invited to organize T.I.E.teams in C.F.C. congregations. About twenty-five young people came from England to join our own folks in evangelism. We had four days training, then split up and dispatched teams to Holywood, Banbridge, Cregagh and Strandtown. It was a powerful time for all those involved. Steve thoroughly enjoyed working in Ireland and looked forward to developing the contacts between our young people.

It was decision time. Was it in God's plan for us to formalize a bond with Pioneer Ministries? I attended a missionary conference in England and was invited by Gerald Coates to stay on. After a meal together, we began to discuss how we saw the future. He gave me an analysis of my character as he might present it to his leadership. He said that in my favour was the absence of any major moral problems, past or present. He described me as a good man with very high standards, concerned about sins which might be overlooked by others. Just one area troubled him, a fear that one day I might simply quit; that without proper support I might suddenly decide that I couldn't cope and walk away from it all. In that event, he warned, I would need friends.

Some people do not like Gerald Coates. I personally really love him. I think he is an inspirational figure, and I 'clicked' with him and responded to his involvement in my life. I was attracted to Pioneer, and believe that Gerald was genuinely concerned about what would happen to the church if for any reason I was off the scene. His words left me not a little shaken, but I was more aware than ever of the differences of perception that existed between us, particularly the belief that models which work in England can be transported across the Irish sea. The Irishman is not simply a more primitive form of the Englishman! The history of C.F.C., particularly the events surrounding the resignations, had formed our beliefs about church. Had we not been reminded in a dramatic way that the church belongs to God? He raises leaders to fulfil his purposes, and none of us can presume to carry an anointing for ever. God requires from us total dependence on Him, and total obedience to His will. He had taught me to hold all things lightly. In the autumn of 1990, we as a leadership took the decision not to go down the Pioneer route. Although we believed in the principle of being under authority, we understood this in a local context. As elders we are submitted to one another, and they are my guard against deception. The idea of trans-local authority did not sit comfortably with us. We were still living with the consequences of the Shepherding Movement.

The Pioneer leaders were proposing to establish long-term T.I E.teams in Belfast, with an emphasis on discipleship training. Steve Clifford was very disappointed when we pulled the plug on this scheme, but we were concerned that Peter Dornan, our youth leader, would be accountable to them. Ultimately it was a question of vision rather than personality. We believed that our focus should be on issues at home and the importance of discovering the role we had to play in the healing of divisions and the extension of God's kingdom in Ireland.

In 1987 Roy Hession, author of the Christian classic, The Calvary Road, came to speak at the church. He spoke on his favourite topic, the amazing grace of God. An old man by then, he was concerned to encourage young people into the ministry of the gospel, and asked me what provision we were making for training. I was honest and said that we had not given much thought to this issue. He was gracious but firm, 'Maybe you better think about it,' he said. Inspired by the example of the Pioneer team in this area, we began to set up our own in-house training teams for our young people. In the summer of 1991, we called them Training in Outreach and Evangelism

(T.O.E.) teams. This was too similar to the Pioneer name, but these teams were a stepping stone into a full-time training programme.

The groups meeting in Banbridge and Holywood had been greatly encouraged by the summer teams working with them. Jim Thompson was becoming more involved in the Cregagh area of East Belfast, and the question of church planting faced us now as a priority issue. As a new church, one of the first things we did together, was to have a week of prayer and fasting. Usually held in the early months of the year, this has remained a regular feature of C.F.C. life. It has always been a significant time for me personally, and has a unifying effect on those who participate. We meet together during the week, both morning and evening, to pray and listen for God's direction. At our first such week in 1990, Alan George delivered a prophetic word on the subject of church planting. God was telling us that He would not give us a map; He wanted His people to follow a guide. We were to hear and do what the Holy Spirit was saying.

In the first instance, planting new churches was left to pioneering individuals. Since the days of Down Christian Trust in Holywood, there had been a vision for a local witness in the town. In 1988 when I asked George Dines to consider establishing a church there, he was reluctant, because of a previous aborted attempt. The time was right, however, and with all their experience, he and Nora make a great team. Theirs is now a thriving congregation, and the first to become autonomous.

Ian and Pamela Mitchell moved to Banbridge in 1987, with the express purpose of ultimately planting a church there. For three years they had a small fellowship in their home, and in 1990 a group of about thirty began to meet on Sunday mornings in a community centre. This number has now grown to around one hundred.

In these early stages, although helped and supported by members from Strandtown, the church planters were out there somewhere doing a good job, but the rest of us were not too concerned about the detail. Meanwhile the Strandtown congregation was growing to nearly unmanageable proportions, with people travelling from further and further afield to fellowship with us. We believed that church planting was God's alternative to buying land and building a 2,000 seater. He was stirring all our hearts to look beyond the relative comfort and security of a thriving congregation, and face up to the needs of a divided province, and Ireland as a whole. Our identity was to be in His purposes, rather than in any agenda of our own. God was calling us to be an evangelising movement, sharing His message of reconciliation and hope, under the banner of His kingdom.

In the summer of 1991, while on holiday, I read Dawn 2000, by Jim Montgomery. The book was a challenge to take seriously the vision of church planting as a means of reaching the world with the gospel. He wrote that every nation requires a John Knox who said, 'Give me Scotland or I die.' When I read those words, I thought, 'That's how I feel about

Ireland.' It was a time of revelation as God gave me a glimpse of the need to reach both sides of the community, if we were ever going to touch this island with His love.

In a country torn apart by civil strife and religious bigotry, there is much resistance to God's desire for a non-sectarian Christianity. Each side of the religious divide believes itself to be 'right,' and hopes for final victory over the other. Anyone preaching peace and forgiveness is viewed with suspicion, and accused of compromise. The Ecumenical Movement attempts to bring people together on the basis of mutual respect for Protestant and Roman Catholic identity. We, however, are not ecumenical, but evangelical. We believe that true unity only exists where Protestant and Roman Catholic kneel together at the cross of Jesus, and allow Him to strip them of their religion and be clothed in His righteousness alone.

I part company here with those only seeking renewal within traditional denominations. While I recognize the integrity of the individual and his right to hold an opinion, this does not preclude an attempt to persuade him of the truth of the gospel. The good news extends beyond a sacrifice for sin to the restoration of a person and a nation, in the power of the Spirit of God. In Northern Ireland we have gospel campaigns and rallies, at the end of which people return to their ghettos. This problem can only be addressed by the establishment of groups of believers in every locality who represent a viable, Spirit-filled, evangelising expression of Church. These must reflect the culture and heritage of the area, in order to defeat the lie that you have to become a Unionist to be a follower of Jesus Christ.

C.F.C. Strandtown stands in a largely Protestant Belfast suburb, but we do not call ourselves a Protestant church. Realistically, however, we draw most of our members from the locality and the surrounding Protestant area of North Down and 'Ards. From the outset, I have been concerned to shake off the Unionist mentality, and more than once God has called us to repentance for the arrogant, bigoted attitudes which surface from time to time. Everyone in Northern Ireland carries around cultural 'baggage,' but we preach allegiance to the kingdom of God, not to any earthly political power.

The week of prayer and fasting in 1992, marked a turning point for the church corporately, and for me personally, as we received challenge after challenge to take seriously our calling to be bridge-builders in a divided land. God was asking us to be willing to invest the much that we had been given in the extension of His kingdom. He rebuked our complacency, and warned us against enjoying our ease. John McGregor, a young man from a Roman Catholic background, working in West Belfast, spoke a word of prophecy, based on Ezekiel's vision of one nation under one king (Ezekiel 37: 15–22). God instructs the prophet to take two sticks, one representing the house of Judah, and the other the house of Joseph, and join them together that they become one in his hand.

'... they will never again be two nations or divided

into two kingdoms... They will be my people and I will be their God.' (v. 22–23) God's word to us was that we had to be prepared to take the initiative; the prophet held the sticks in his hand, then God took charge. He said that the country was watching, and that the time had come for us to put into practice our vision for non-sectarian Christianity. We have the resources and the gifts to take the hands of others and draw them together. John's point was that God is looking for spiritual, rather than political unity. Where people are open to welcome one another in His Name, the Father says, 'I will make a covenant of peace with them.'(v.27) I received a personal charge to prepare the congregation for the years ahead. Two issues were going to come to the fore. Firstly we believed that we were called to reach Ireland through planting new churches. All of us, including me, had to be willing to be thrust out from Strandtown, if that was what God required in order to fulfil the vision. This raised all sorts of questions about training and preparation. In our foundation course for new members, our desire to plant churches is explained and people are encouraged to be open to God's leading on this matter. Not everyone will leave Strandtown, however, and the second question to be addressed, was how to develop the congregation as a resource centre. God impressed on us the importance of the church in Belfast as a base for training in all areas of leadership and ministry.

Following the week of prayer and fasting, the elders carefully considered all the prophetic words that had

been delivered, and felt that the time had come for clarification. In 1987, I had outlined a five-year plan for church growth. This had been realized beyond our expectations, and it was now time to establish a framework for the years ahead, including defining the vision, and setting out how God was leading us towards its fulfilment. Some of the new issues to be addressed were presented to members as a twenty point plan:
1. To plant 400 new churches in Ireland by 2010 A.D.
2. To plant 5 new local C.F.C.s by September 1994.
3. To plant a church in Dublin during 1995.
4. To release 5% of total offerings into a separate church planting fund during 1992.

Task teams to be established in the following areas by June 1993:
5. Evangelism
6. Social Action
7. Teaching
8. Healing/Ministry
9. Prophetic
10. Pastoral Care
11. Reconciliation
12. Church Planting
13. T.E.A.M. Project to be started by October 1992.
14. Esther Smyrle to be come part-time youth worker in May 1992.
15. To see average giving rise to £22,000 per month by the end of 1993.
16. To pay existing debt (£300,000) by the end of

1995.
17. To buy the house beside the church during 1992.
18. To see 100 new converts by June 1993.
19. To have a Church Planting conference in the Ulster Hall by June 1993.
20. To plant a church in Europe during 1997.

Several of these goals have been achieved in full. The Task teams are well underway, engaged in training in specific areas of ministry, the Ulster Hall rally was held in March 1993, and former social worker, Esther Smyrle, is now a full-time member of staff. The house next door has been purchased, totally through generous gifts from members. This has become the base for the first intake to our one year Training in Evangelism and Ministry (T.E.A.M.) Project, administered by Peter Dornan, who, along with Clifford Kennedy, was ordained an elder in 1991.

The aim of the project is two-fold:
1. To help the eight young men and women who have enrolled to develop personally.
2. To use them in evangelism in new church plant situations.

They will be active in church life for thirty weeks of the year, both at Strandtown and in the sister churches. The remaining weeks will be taken up with training blocks. In these they will receive systematic Bible teaching, examine the issues which face the Church today, and learn how to manage time, pray effectively and share their faith. They will participate in the national Together for the Kingdom conference, and also have a two-week trip overseas. These young people are not in training to become full-time workers in the church, this is training for life.

Not everyone is happy with the concept of planting new churches. There will always be people who think on a purely local level, but everyone is being encouraged to discover his or her part in what God is doing among us. The opportunities to develop and use the gifts given to us by God, are tremendous. The lack of a blueprint worries some, but it is the Holy Spirit who plants churches!

7

From Ireland to India

The trouble with being led by the Spirit, is that it can be untidy in human terms. To date there are five C.F.C. congregations. These have sprung up in a variety of ways, but there are issues common to all: the need for a clear vision, the appointment of strong leadership, the importance of committed members and the defining of the area and people to be reached.

In C.F.C., we do not have a written constitution. Our statement of faith makes clear what we believe, but it does not account for how we do things. On a personal level, I cannot conduct my ministry on any other basis than good relationships. The old adage about written agreements, 'Good men don't need them and bad men don't keep them,' is my philosophy. This frequently opens us up to abuse and leaves us vulnerable, but we find God often honours our willingness to take risks. There is, however, a distinctive feel about C.F.C. churches, and I believe that there are ten things which characterize us:

1. An emphasis on praise and worship.
2. The centrality of prayer and the Word of God.
3. An obvious ministry of the Holy Spirit.
4. The importance of relationships.
5. A focus on Body ministry and the priesthood of all believers.
6. A heart for evangelism, reaching the lost and planting them into new churches.
7. A world vision with involvement in overseas mission.
8. A concern for the poor and disadvantaged and a desire for social justice.
9. A prophetic voice to the nation, proclaiming non-sectarian Christianity.
10. The unity of all believers, regardless of church affiliation.

There is an ethos, not always communicable verbally, rather received in the Spirit. We have all drunk from the same barrel, and depend on that oneness in the Spirit to communicate throughout towns and villages what God has entrusted to us. How then do we answer the charge that there are enough churches in Ireland? This is often levelled at us in Northern Ireland, where a church building or mission hall occupies a place of importance in every townland, and where denominational allegiance is jealously guarded. It is usually those whose first loyalty is to a particular denomination, who are most threatened at the prospect of a new one. If denominations are so dangerous, what are they doing in one? And if they are essential, the more the merrier! It has been estimated that the world will only be reached with the gospel, when every person has access to an evangelising, culturally relevant church. This would require one church for every 1,500–2,000 people in rural areas, and one for every 1,000 people in the town. According to these figures, we don't have nearly enough churches in Ireland. We still need 2,500 more! Roger Forster tells the story of how their much loved family dog was ill and on its last legs. In anticipation of the impact of the loss of their pet, Roger and his wife bought a puppy for their daughter. The introduction of young blood had an amazing effect on the old dog. Rather than taking it as his cue to move on, he began to revive and found a new lease of life. So it is with churches. Wherever a new church is planted in an area, everyone benefits. The reason for this is three-fold. Firstly, as Roger Forster's story vividly illustrates, languishing congregations sit up, take notice, and are challenged to change. Then there is an upsurge of general gospel awareness. Finally, and most significantly, the presence in an area of a group of people active in spiritual warfare, begins to tear down Satan's strongholds and releases blessings from on high.

In my opinion, one of the factors which inhibited growth in the old fellowship days, was a desire for perfection. Everything had to be just right before anything was attempted. God delivered us from this and liberated us into a simple belief that if we were obedient to His voice, He would take care of the consequences. His word to us was, 'Freely you have received, freely give.' Our practice has been to take risks, allow the Spirit room to move and restrain ourselves from pruning the bush too early. This may be in part a reaction to the control of the past, but ours is a God of variety, and it is exciting to see Him at work in different ways. He promises to guide, and all He asks from us is availability and obedience.

The label of denomination is neither here nor there. God is at work in Ireland. We see ample evidence of this Sunday after Sunday in our packed church at Strandtown. Many people from every tradition, and none, come forward for prayer each week. Some decide to stay, that they may continue to receive the on-going ministry of the Holy Spirit in their lives. In the twentieth century, with the advent of the family car, we measure distance not in miles, but in minutes. We live in one location, work in another and worship somewhere else. People travel to Strandtown from far and wide, and many are happy to do so. Full involvement in church life is difficult, however, especially mid-week.

Over the years home groups have been established in all areas where C.F.C. people live. These provide the opportunity for fellowship, Bible study and ministry in the Body of Christ. In some of the outlying towns, there are several such groups. When the numbers attending regularly reach thirty or forty, the question arises as to whether this could form the nucleus of a church plant. I am a firm believer in the local church. I think Spirit-filled Christians need to establish a witness where they live.

As we work towards the goal of 400 new churches in Ireland by the year 2010, we will be planting in three different contexts. Ultimately we will move into the South, starting with Dublin. To this end we are praying for God to call people with a heart for Roman Catholics, and an ability to bridge the cultural gap, working alongside people already on the ground.

Also in Northern Ireland, we hope to face the challenge of planting new churches in predominantly Roman Catholic areas. Amazing as it may seem, this has seldom been done, although there are small pockets of Spirit-filled believers throughout the province. One of our members, Paddy McGlinchey, born in the Roman Catholic area of 'Derry known as the Bogside, recently encouraged me in this. He said that the reason he came to C.F.C. was that there was nothing in our church life which threatened his cultural identity; he didn't have to change his politics to become a member.

Initially, however, our focus has been on Protestant East Belfast and the surrounding suburbs, simply because we draw most of our folks from this locality. I believe that we are witnessing a fresh surge of interest in the things of the Spirit within mainline Protestant denominations. People are tired of religion and are searching for the abundant life promised by Jesus. Evidence of this can be seen in the numbers of people attending Spring Harvest and the Belfast Youth For Christ monthly rally, Mannafest. We can sing

Graham Kendrick songs, re-arrange the chairs, and even bring in a band, but without an outpouring of the Holy Spirit in our churches, religious activity remains lifeless. God is eager to baptize His children with power from on high and gifts to equip His Church, but there is such a fear on the part of Protestant clergy that somehow the Holy Spirit might begin to operate outside traditional boundaries, that He is quenched, and a grieving results in the hearts of those who are thirsty.

As a consequence of this, C.F.C. inherits Christians with a solid evangelical base, who are looking for a new relationship with the Lord through the person of the Holy Spirit. I do not want to get caught up in terminology, but I firmly believe that the step from a vague awareness of the Holy Spirit as the third person of the Godhead, into a dynamic, vital relationship with the Holy Spirit as one who anoints with power and fills to overflowing, is a quantum leap. Many of us who thought we knew the Holy Spirit, found that we only knew about Him. He is God, yet He reveals the mysteries of God to us. He was a gift from the Father yet He showers us with gifts. Revival will only come to our Protestant churches when religion gives way to the working of the Holy Spirit.

In C.F.C. 50% of our growth can be accounted for by transfers from other churches. Some who are in a back-slidden state, experience a personal revival and move on to a place where they want to reach out to others. We do not deliberately set out to steal sheep, nor do we turn them away. Our Sunday Night at

C.F.C. meetings were started as an evangelistic outreach, and to encourage our own folks in the ministries of the Holy Spirit. However, we also see the meetings as a resource to the whole Church. We occasionally send teams in to local churches to conduct seminars on the Holy Spirit, and are happy to continue to do so, but I believe that in Ireland those situations where the operations of the Holy Spirit have been contained within a denominational context, are exceptions rather than the rule.

25,000 people live within the borough of Carrickfergus. A recent survey estimates that 2,500 attend church on a Sunday. If all the churches were full, they could fit in another 2,500 people. That still leaves 20,000 unreached folk, and this in a town boasting twenty-seven churches. We reckon that there is room for one more at least! C.F.C. Carrick is our latest church planting project. In 1986 we inherited a semi-autonomous fellowship, linked in with Down Christian Trust. After the resignations, it fell apart and those who remained became a C.F.C. housegroup. Out of that emerged potential leaders, and in 1992 we recognized that God had annointed Bill and Margaret Roy for the task of establishing a witness in the area. A group has been meeting on Sundays since the beginning of 1993.

Sometimes if you start with a housegroup mentality, it takes a long time to turn it round. This is not the case in Bangor, however, where 95% of the forty people in housegroups, are very keen to become a church plant. Bangor is the third largest town in

Northern Ireland. Protestant, middle class and undergoing major development, Bangor has suffered in recent months from terrorist bomb attacks. We are praying that a clear leader will emerge, who can carry the challenge of a new church there. Before we start to build a local congregation, I prefer to know who the leaders are, but we are eager to move forward, take risks, respond to what God is already doing, and see His kingdom advanced.

In our three established local congregations, the leaders came first. Elder Jim Thompson and his wife Kitty have been working in the Cregagh area of East Belfast since 1990. They have a heart for the poor, and established their witness through reaching out to those who were hurting and in need. Their personal courage and faith when a tumour threatened the eye-sight of their three year old daughter, Alison, has been a great blessing to all those who know them.

In the initial stages, leaders are appointed but the eldership is retained by Strandtown, until such time as there is a plurality of elders in the local congregation. A Ministry Team has been formed to maintain a forward momentum in church planting and oversee new congregations. The members of this team are all elders in Strandtown and the sister churches, and our role is to stir up the gifts of evangelist, prophet, pastor and teacher, vital to the birth of a local church. It is our responsibility to ensure the laying of good foundations in teaching and practice, and to encourage leaders, who often feel isolated.

During the first two years in Holywood, authority

was delegated to George Dines, and he received help and support from Strandtown. After this time, on George's personal recommendation, Michael Paul was considered for eldership. He also gained the approval of the members of the congregation and was interviewed by the elders. Subsequently the Ministry Team went to Holywood, laid hands on Michael and ordained him as an elder. He and George were commissioned as the leaders of Holywood C.F.C., and later Paul Betts joined the eldership team. Those of us most closely involved have taken a step back, and my role has become that of older brother rather than father. We maintain a good relationship, but direct involvement is by invitation only.

Like Carrickfergus, Newtownards is well-churched, but God spoke clearly when a young man from the town, Stephen Smyth, joined our foundation course. During a prayer meeting, the Holy Spirit prompted me to speak a prophetic word to him from John 15:16 'You did not choose me, but I chose you to go and bear fruit.' I said that God had brought him to Strandtown where he would find a home, but that it was a launching pad for service elsewhere. God was calling him into church planting. Two housegroups have started in Newtownards, and Stephen and Catherine are looking forward to the day when these will grow into a church.

God told us that we would grow some churches ourselves, while others would be grafted in. Our church plants to date have developed in different ways, and we are discovering that the initiative will not always be taken by us. Brian Baird, an ex-Elim pastor leading a fellowship in Coleraine, came down to Belfast, liked what he found, and asked if his fellowship could become a C.F.C. congregation. As I considered this, God reminded me of the word to 'freely give,' and encouraged me to share both our ethos and our vision. Brian has a burden to ultimately reach out into 'Derry and Donegal. I suggested that we take a few steps round the dance floor first, to see if we are comfortable together, before we announce an engagement.

Religious groups which are here today and gone tomorrow, are viewed with great suspicion in Northern Ireland, so we have tended to make the acquisition of buildings a priority as evidence of our commitment to an area. To date, none of our local leaders is working for the church full-time. As regards on-going oversight of the increasing number of congregations, we still believe that there is no higher authority than that of elder. This conclusion was reached after consideration of other models of government, specifically the prevalent perception of the role of apostle as the chief in a hierarchy. I believe in modern day apostles, but I think that they are essentially different from the originals. The word apostle means 'sent out one,' and Jesus is described as the 'apostle of our faith,' sent from heaven to fulfil the Father's purpose. An apostle today does not collect churches, he plants them. His is an extra-local role, and he should only be involved in the business of a local congregation when invited. We may eventually have to set up oversight teams to cover specific areas, but, in the meantime, all matters regarding our new congregations will be handled by the C.F.C. Ministry Team.

In 1992 we had a visit from an Assemblies of God youth pastor, Mike Lindquist, working in South America. He originally made contact through a mutual friend because he wanted to send over a group of his young people to do mission service in Ireland. The young people, many of Mexican extraction, came and a relationship developed between our churches. On this his second visit, Mike spoke prophetically a message which he believed God had given to him for our situation. In essence it was, 'Go for the world and I will give you the city.' We received this as from the Lord and as confirmation that we were to plant churches beyond Ireland. We began to expand our vision and our slogan became, 'Change the world through church planting.' As regards church planting overseas, the main thrust of our work is in India. The basis for this involvement is in the moving story of Alan and Janet George's longing for a child. In 1985 a World Intercessors' Conference was held in Northern Ireland, at which Derek Prince was the main speaker. Hospitality was given to delegates at the conference by members of the Bangor fellowship. Thus Alan and Janet met an Indian pastor called N.John Wilson. He became very interested in their desire to be parents, and offered to pursue the possibility of them adopting an Indian baby.

At that time John Wilson had established around

twenty churches, an orphanage and a school under the banner of the United Christian Church of India. In 1986 he died and his son N.John Winston took over the work. In that same year, Alan George and Hugh Jervis went to India, where Alan met a baby girl, chosen for him and Janet by John Wilson in 1985, and still in the care of his family. Many of the children in the orphanage are not in fact orphans; in most cases their parents are too poor to care for them at home, but their families keep in touch. This little girl was different. Her parents abandoned her because in India daughters are of little value, and she was one too many.

With adoption procedures underway, a vital contact was made with a group of people eager to plant churches, but with few resources. God gave us a burden for this work and from 1987 we covenanted 10% of the church's income to overseas mission. Individuals and couples began to sponsor children in the orphanage, and this number has now risen to over eighty. Furthermore since that time, teams from the church have visited India regularly to conduct training seminars and larger meetings.

The work has grown over the years. In Kathlaconda, a miracle happened when a Hindu released a plot of land at a reasonable price. In 1989 I was among a team of twenty who went out to lay the foundation stone of this new work. It was a time of political unrest in the area, and one day we spent twenty-three hours under curfew. £30,000 was donated by C.F.C. members and a school, an orphanage and a church were built. We believe that our role is to help John Winston by providing resources both human and financial, but the work is his, not ours. We count it a privilege to share in what God is doing on the continent of India, where there is an unprecedented openness to the gospel, and new congregations of believers are being established throughout the country.

In 1990, during a visit to the church by the Wimber team, Paul Cain delivered a specific word of prophecy to Janet George. He said that he could see her wearing a maternity dress, that the pregnancy had lasted five years and that God had given her a grace-package. Two months earlier, Alan and Janet had brought home their beautiful Indian daughter. It was five years since she had been first chosen for them, and they had given her the name, Grace.

Reach the Unreached, is the name of an evangelistic movement in Kenya established in 1990 by another C.F.C. couple, Richard and Agnes Gunning. Their main emphasis is on large gospel crusades and training seminars for native pastors and church elders. The work in Kenya is marked by the amazing miracles which accompany the preaching of the gospel. Richard has witnessed the blind seeing, the deaf hearing, the dumb speaking and cripples walking. In 1992 churches were planted in Wamba and Maralal, two of the places first visited by the Gunnings.

Other people supported by C.F.C. overseas, include Gary and Helen Sloan working with Operation

Mobilisation in Eastern Europe. They have recently moved to St. Petersburg, where they establishing a new witness. Many of our members have at some time worked with Youth With A Mission, and at present Jane Bambrick is based in Amsterdam. For four months in 1992, she was involved in planting a church in the city of Krasnoyarsk, in Siberia. She tells of the excitement of seeing a Christian witness established in a region closed to the outside world for so long. She echoes God's call for the Church to extend her borders, 'Enlarge the place of your tent, stretch your tent curtains wide, do not hold back; lengthen your cords, strengthen your stakes. For you will spread out to the right and to the left; your descendants will dispossess nations and settle in desolate cities.' (Isaiah 54:2&3) Since the prophecy delivered by Mike Lindquist, we have been praying that God would open up other fields of service as well as India and Kenya, where we can invest time, money and people. We believe that we need to continually reach into new areas, rather than merely sustain what we are already doing.

Church planting does not come with a guarantee of success. Our enjoyment of taking risks may one day lead to disappointment. Jesus chose Judas to be His disciple, in the knowledge that he would one day betray Him and split the team. The goal is not the expansion of C.F.C., but the extension of the kingdom of God. What is the key for leadership at this time of many changes? While travelling by 'plane, I love to see the pilot chatting to the passengers, but during take-off and landing, I want to know that he is behind the controls! Similarly when things are going well in a church, and even more so when things are going badly, people are happy with strong directive leadership. In the main, however, a sharing, consultative type of leadership is required. In some respects, we are in a new 'take-off' period at Strandtown, as people adjust to the implications of embracing the church planting vision. At present, my place is here co-ordinating the work in the city of Belfast I love so much, but I too have to be listening to the voice of the Holy Spirit if a call comes to move on. Whatever the consequences, my prayer is, 'Give me Ireland, or I'll bust!'

8

Together for the Kingdom

Since the resignations and subsequent restoration of the church at Strandtown, God had been opening our spiritual eyes to look beyond the confines of East Belfast. Most of us had known nothing but civil strife and sectarian violence from our youth. It was time to begin to discover whether we had a role in communicating God's message of hope, peace and reconciliation, across the religious divide. We began to wait before the Lord, and a love for our war-torn country was renewed. As we emerged from the wilderness, we realized that it was harvest time and God was looking for workers

As the new leader in C.F.C., I was asked to join the house church leaders fraternity. Paul Kyle (Community of the King), Robert Mearns (Laos Fellowship), Derek Poole (Greenfield Community, Portadown), Carl Hecox and David Kidd (City Church) were meeting for mutual encouragement and fellowship. They were responsible for organizing several conferences, including one with Derek Prince. The group was beginning to lose momentum, however, and as the new boy, I found it difficult to fit in. Eventually the fellowship broadened its base to include some Methodist ministers, but things started to dissolve when the, 'Why are we doing this?' debate began. The final collapse of this group followed a few months later

Meanwhile in C.F.C., we were praying about the way forward as we tried to forget the past and move on in God's purposes for us. Tired of our own self-righteousness, and that of the House Church Movement at large, we began to make overtures to the traditional churches. We wanted to extend a hand of friendship to those whom we had antagonized in the past. Significant in this regard, was the formation in Northern Ireland of the Evangelical Alliance. The aim of this organization is to promote unity among those with an evangelical perspective, and to come together on issues that affect society. Clive Calver, general director of E.A., formed a local executive committee. My inclusion on this committee as the house church representative, was important as we tried to broaden our credibility in relation to the mainline denominations. I took active steps to meet leaders from other churches, and I was not so long out of evangelical circles that they had forgotten I was 'sound.' However, in Northern Ireland you can't win. My involvement with the evangelicals soon led to accusations from other house churches that I was too conservative. The charge of extreme evangelicalism was more perceived than real. I had not betrayed my new found joy and freedom in the Holy Spirit; my stance was merely a reflection of what I am. Since my baptism in the Holy Spirit, I redefine myself as a charismatic evangelical, not an evangelical charismatic. I am evangelical first and foremost, and charismatic second in history, experience and theology. Finding out where we fitted in between the traditional church and the other new churches, meant walking a fine line

My friendship with Clive Calver, through involvement with the Evangelical Alliance, opened the door for me to return to Spring Harvest, this time as a speaker. In 1990 I shared a seminar with Garth Hewitt, and surprised him by whispering, 'Give them hell!' just before he spoke. This was an old joke from my Brethren days when I used to encourage my father-in-law with the same words, as he left to preach at a meeting

I spoke at Spring Harvest several times over the next few years on many subjects, and was interested to see the renewal of the Church in a British context. God was establishing a strong base for us in Strandtown, however, and my roots were firmly planted in Irish soil

There had been a reshuffle among the house church leaders in the North, as some of them went through their own crises. A smaller group comprising Derek Poole, George Hilary (Lisburn Christian Fellowship) and Andy McCarroll (City Church) started to meet on an ad hoc basis for prayer and fellowship. I joined them in 1989 and we began to look seriously at what the house churches had to say, if anything, to the whole Church in Ireland. Our own relationships were fragile, but we recognized the need to be part of what God was doing nationally

Some years earlier, I had met Niall Barry, a church leader from Dublin. Niall has a broader ministry to the Church through the anti-abortion organization, L.I.F.E. and evangelistic and training work in Africa, as well as heading Kingdom Life Fellowship in the city. He is also on the T.E.A.R. Fund advisory board, of which I am Vice Chairman. In March 1990, Niall and I renewed our acquaintance at Together for the Nation, a jamboree in Sheffield, organized by Gerald Coates and Roger Forster. I remember leaning across to him and saying, 'Why don't we do something like Spring Harvest in Ireland?' Niall was excited at the thought, and immediately Mosney Holiday Camp in Co.Meath came to mind as the obvious venue

The leaders of the New Churches in the South were already planning their own event together, and were streets ahead of us in terms of relationship. Niall and I set up a meeting to discuss the feasibility of a cross-border event, and we each brought four people. I took Hugh Jervis, fellow elder in C.F.C., and Andy, Derek and George from the other house churches. The seeds were sown, but as we drove home to the North, we agreed that we had very little experience of co-operation with each other. A major conference in the South was developing as a real possibility for

Easter 1992, so we decided to hold our own week-end holiday/conference by way of preparation in Castlewellan, Co.Down in June 1991. As we planned the conference, we began to build relationship with each other and in the event, everything went well. Speakers included Rev. Ken Newell from Fitzroy Presbyterian Church, Belfast and Rev. Jim Rea from the East Belfast Mission. It was a time of frolic and fellowship and attracted many young people. 'Next stop Mosney!' I thought, but there were more differences between us than we had realized

After the next meeting with our fellow leaders in the South, first Derek Poole and then Andy McCaroll decided to withdraw from the planning committee of the cross border conference. Each had his own reasons, but I was deeply distressed by their decisions. Together for the Kingdom, was the name chosen for the first all-Ireland conference of its kind, and now it looked like, 'almost Together for the Kingdom,' would be more appropriate. I was annoyed that amidst all the talk of reconciliation, it appeared that Ulstermen can't work with anybody. I felt that these two brothers were isolating themselves and was grieved. It was the end of the four of us as a fellowship group, although Derek was later to make a significant contribution as a seminar speaker at Mosney

Executive committee members in the South included Graeme Wylie (an Ulsterman leading a church in Galway), Gary Davidson (from the U.S.A. working in St. Mark's, Dublin), Mark Hapgood (a New Zealander, from Maranatha Fellowship, Dublin),

Niall Barry and P.J.McKenna (Dublin). Joe Kelly (St. Mark's) was added to this team after the death of P.J.McKenna. We brought in Barry White (Coleraine Christian Fellowship) and Noel Mills (then Dromore Elim, now Westport, Co.Mayo) and the preparations for Together for the Kingdom got underway

Recognizing the pull of Spring Harvest, we sought advice from Clive Calver. Initially he was alarmed at the prospect of an Irish conference at Easter, because of the threat to their own week in Ayr, traditionally attended by large numbers from Northern Ireland. Long-term their sights were on mainland Europe, however, and we felt that our desire to reach folks south of the Irish border, justified a Spring conference. Peter Meadows and Colin Saunders, both on the Spring Harvest executive committee, came over and were very supportive in our planning efforts. Once the final decision to go ahead had been made, Hugh Jervis went to England and benefited greatly from their experience in the administration of such a venture. Hugh took on the major part of the organization of Together for the Kingdom. He is a brillant administrator. I come up with the idea and Hugh tells me why I can't do it! There were decisions to be made with regard to defining our vision. Everyone was agreed that a cross-border evangelical conference was an idea whose time was ripe. For many it had been a dream for which they had prayed, but in order to see it fulfilled, practical issues had to be addressed. The most difficult of these was whether to broaden the committee base to include evangelicals of a charismatic nature from mainline denominations, at the planning stage. We took advice from Roger Forster, a leader from Ichthus Christian Fellowship, London on this question. He said that we should not have people on committee purely by way of representation, but on the basis of relationship. We decided, therefore, to establish a New Church ethos for the conference. This stance was not without its critics, but our experience had already proved how difficult it could be to make united progress with leaders we knew. Our vision for Ireland was, One new man in Christ, and our aim, finally, was two-fold:

1. To envision the new churches to establish their own ethos and develop a church planting agenda
2. To encourage mainline denominations into a greater openness to the work of the Holy Spirit, and to build them up

These aims sprang from an awareness that we in the House Church Movement were facing new challenges. Having received the initial vision of fresh praise and worship, committed relationships, community living, and freedom in the Holy Spirit, we had to find the way to channel outwards, in service to the whole Body of Christ, and in evangelism. At the same time, it was important to recognize that there is something distinctive about new churches. We wanted to be secure enough to say, 'This is what we believe, and it's worth believing.' We had occasion to praise God in the months that followed that many of our contacts in the mainline denominations, north and south, were not too offended to accept invitations to speak at the conference, and the programme began to take shape. It was important to welcome others to Mosney as speakers and contributors, who were working in areas unexplored by us

One such was Rev. Ken Newell from Fitzroy Presbyterian Church in Belfast. Ken involves himself in cross community Bible studies in very troubled parts of the city, and has had more experience than most of bringing God's reconciling love to lives devastated by terrorist violence. He expressed the belief that the vision for Together for the Kingdom embraced the Easter themes of joy, unity and humility. His comments were prophetic: 'There will be many signs of unity as we witness the bonding that is taking place in Ireland between disciples of Jesus, who, after centuries of political bitterness and spiritual apartheid, now know they are one family with one heavenly Father. There will be a spirit of true humility as those from the historic churches learn from the new churches the lessons of confidence and power, and as those from the new churches learn from the mainline churches the lessons of stability and faithfulness. There will be an attempt to face with courage the real issues of life in Ireland north and south today; they will not be ducked but faced with honesty. We will see a vision of an alternative Ireland, an alternative Ulster, where Jesus is King, where every life is sacred, where justice and peace have embraced, and where the love of Christ pervades God's Easter people and generates a warmer environment for the whole of society.' Initially we expected

TOGETHER FOR THE KINGDOM

1,500 people, mostly from Northern Ireland. The registration forms poured in, however, and the week's conference was booked out before Christmas. We had to negotiate extra accommodation with the owners of Mosney. One Englishwoman travelling from the North, was fully expecting to see pigs in the kitchen in the south of Ireland, and when we saw the basic chalets, we could almost believe it ourselves. Easter 1992 was very cold and wet. Undeterred, people came – 2,500 of them, and amazingly 50/50 from north and south. From initial planning to final celebration, God was at work in a mighty way

Our main emphasis was on home-grown talent, male and female, north and south. Most of the speakers and all of the musicians were from churches in Ireland. An exception was made in the case of Tom Bathgate, who gave the morning Bible readings from the book of Daniel. Tom is passionately Scottish, but is now based in Calvary Christian Fellowship, Preston, Lancashire. He was invited on the strength of his commitment to Ireland, having worked in a church in the North for several years. Tom was thrilled to hear about the vision of Together for the Kingdom. His first words were, 'Well done, God!' Tom's teaching was inspired, both in the mornings and at an evening celebration. He said that at the conference there was an awareness of the presence of God in power, that he had not experienced elsewhere

Other main event speakers included Roger Forster, Ben Tipton, Niall Barry and myself. Our theme was Together for the Kingdom, and our unity was demonstrated in our ability to work towards the common goal of exalting the name of Jesus Christ above our differences. In seminars throughout the day we examined many practical, and sometimes controversial, aspects of kingdom living

The week was dedicated to the memory of P.J.McKenna, a member of the executive committee who died suddenly in the autumn of 1991, on the day after a very happy time of fellowship with the rest of the team. P.J. was forty-four, and his wife Honor was left with five children, the youngest only a few weeks old. P.J. was totally committed to the vision of Together for the Kingdom, and Honor was a great source of blessing to all who attended in her courageous leadership of the children's work at the conference

Coming from all corners, and from behind denominational walls, Christians enjoyed united celebration with people whose history differed from theirs, some for the first time. Those who attended from the North and South experienced a sense of togetherness as we worshipped the Lord in harmony, and as we worked alongside each other for the good of the whole. Individuals were prepared to sacrifice personal prejudices for the sake of unity. Many appreciated the opportunity to hear in the seminars what Irish men and women have to say on a variety of subjects. Those from isolated fellowship groups in the South particularly benefited from access to the resources available in books and tapes, and horizons were broadened through visits to the exhibition hall

For all, the conference was a source of great encouragement. This was especially true of the small fellowships who got a sense of being part of something bigger. Gospel hardened Northerners were amazed to meet young Christians hungry for consistent Bible teaching. In the last decade pockets of Christians in the South have paid a high price, many as a result of leaving the Roman Catholic Church. An opportunity to worship and study God's Word with believers from all over the island, renewed their faith and provided hope that God's people can be a force for change in Ireland. We met folks thirsty from lack of fellowship, who were drinking deep draughts of life in the evening celebrations. It wasn't all big hype, however, as a large part of the programme was devoted to the challenge of applying the principles of kingdom living in everyday life. Southern believers living in isolation were introduced to other Christians from the same area, and the way was paved for the establishment of new fellowship groups. Gary Davidson saw God's promise to him furthered as he shared his vision at Mosney, and he has since opened a Bible College/Conference Centre in Greystones, Co.Wicklow

Together for the Kingdom was a warning to Satan, 'writ large.' Old divisions between Christians north and south were beginning to heal. It was significant also in terms of spiritual warfare because it demonstrated a greater gathering of troops in preparation for serious battle, to take the land for Christ and his kingdom. The enemy received a second body blow the following month, when 36,000 people gathered over three nights in the Point Theatre, Dublin to hear teacher and evangelist, Luis Palau. The Roman Catholic establishment and traditional Protestant churches were rattled because the event was organized and supported by New Churches in the South. As these New Churches gain credibility, accusations of cult status have come from Roman Catholic bishops. In our hands are the opportunity and responsibility to demonstrate the kingdom of God in love and with power

Although the ethos of Together for the Kingdom was primarily that of the New Churches, we received many letters of appreciation from Christians within mainline denominations, Baptist, Presbyterian and Roman Catholic, whose lives had been touched and radically changed by the Holy Spirit. Some began, 'I was initially very sceptical, but....' God is turning the hearts of His people towards one another, to fulfil the prayer of Jesus that we serve Him as one

In 1992 we emphasized the importance of togetherness as we serve the King. At the 1993 conference, we will explore the coming of the kingdom. As we face the challenge to take the gospel to every quarter, our prayer will be in the words of Jesus: 'Your kingdom come, Your will be done on earth, as it is in heaven.' (Matthew 6:10)

9

Pushy Northerners

When John Wimber visited Dublin, he described Ireland as, 'darker than the darkest country I've been to,' yet we have one of the most religious societies in the world. In the North we consider ourselves blessed with a strong evangelical heritage, firmly rooted in the Word of God, emphasizing new birth in Christ and the priesthood of all believers. In many churches, however, abundant life is being swallowed up by self-righteous legalism.

Satan has bound many in the south of Ireland by a fear of man. Since the days of the penal laws, there have been generations born with few opportunities in land ownership, business or the church. The Roman Catholic hierarchy has a tremendous hold on people, and this gives rise to resentments, while at the same time preventing individuals from taking personal responsibility. These basic instincts which characterize a nation, must be understood by Christians coming to Ireland from different backgrounds. Only the love of God, an allegiance to His kingdom and the power of the Holy Spirit to heal and restore, can ever overcome the problems in attempting to unite believers north and south on this island.

Our declared aim in Together for the Kingdom, is to encourage the planting of new churches throughout Ireland. We are convinced of the need for every person to have access to a local, evangelical expression of Church, if the island is to be reached with the message of the gospel. To this end there is an urgent need for Protestants and Roman Catholics to acknowledge the stifling effects of religion and step out into freedom in Jesus Christ.

One criticism heard after Together for the Kingdom, 1992 was that, 'The pushy Northerners took over again.' This accusation had some truth in it, as the greater part of resources in terms of finance, skills and personnel came from the North. For decades, Ulstermen have been resented. They have crossed the border bringing Protestant culture, a Protestant religion and standards, and a Protestant ethos. There have been attempts to impose these on the Southerners without any effort to understand them. The label, 'pushy Northerners' is more often used by those Christians in the South who have been struggling for years. As pioneers, they have suffered most and have the greatest fear of control and colonialism. Only a mighty work of God can allow us to overcome centuries of prejudice and set us free to offer and receive forgiveness. We who live in the North and have a vision for planting new churches, must begin to recognize the sensitivities of those who may not welcome born-again raiders from across the border. We must lay aside our Protestant identity and go only in the name of Jesus and in the power of the Holy Spirit, willing to humble ourselves to listen and learn.

Sadly, however, I have discovered that when it comes to organizing events on a national scale, there is a real dearth of experienced speakers and leaders in the south of Ireland. We hope to close this gap by holding leadership conferences in the future, to encourage young men and women with gifts in this area to be confident in who they are in God. Until such times as more leaders in the South are raised up, we believe that we must be willing to serve our brothers and sisters with whatever resources God has blessed us. We want Together for the Kingdom to be for the Irish, by the Irish.

Throughout a large part of Ireland, there is a real need for the preaching of the gospel of regeneration. Many in the South are willing to receive ministry from the platform, but reluctant to embrace Christ's teachings with their power to transform lives, and in turn make them ministers of His truth and life. Learning to take personal responsibility in spiritual matters, and submit to one another in the Body are still new to many southern believers. This gives rise to a strange paradox. Having rejected the priest, who was authoritarian and discouraged the lay man from interpreting the Bible for himself, new Christians have difficulty in accepting any authority. This partially accounts for the leadership struggles which plague the New Churches. There is a looking to foreigners to do something, belying a deep-seated resentment of them, 'Why do we have to depend on you?' In the South there is a real concern on the part of some evangelicals about rocking the Roman Catholic boat. In their efforts to halt the rise of the New Churches, the Roman Catholic Church will most likely attempt to absorb them into the Ecumenical Movement. Some Protestant clergy have already taken this route, and thereby retain their status and acceptable front in society. Resistance remains to those who, while renouncing Roman Catholicism, do not embrace Protestantism, but find fellowship with like-minded people outside the traditional churches. This is more true in the South than in the North, where fellowships are tolerated.

Not all evangelicals in the South are prepared to give support to Together for the Kingdom. The establishment of an Irish Evangelical Alliance was blocked by fundamentalists insisting that no member could have associations with March for Jesus. The Dublin March for Jesus was celebrated in recent years by a hotch-potch of devout church-goers from every conceivable background, reflecting the extremely religious make-up of society. Events with an ecumenical flavour are viewed with great suspicion by those concerned with preserving reformed truth, and Together for the Kingdom has attracted its share of criticism. I am, however, unashamedly evangelical, and while I can co-exist happily with Roman Catholic Christians, God has given me a vision for churches which do not owe an allegiance to either tradition.

In the south of Ireland at present, there are about 10,000 evangelicals in a population of 3.5 million. A significant number of their leaders come from the North or further afield. This is as true in the mainline Protestant denominations as in the New Churches. In Kilkenny Presbyterian Church, Rev.John Woodside and his co-worker Billy Patterson of the Irish Mission, are both from Northern Ireland. They operate a very successful programme of aggressive evangelism. Billy, a 'hard man' from Carryduff, who played football for Distillery, sees no problem for a northern Protestant working among Roman Catholics in the South. He says that when God replaces prejudice with His love, people discern your heart, and accent becomes irrelevant.

As the leader of C.F.C., I have received a charge to pursue the vision of planting non-sectarian churches throughout Ireland. This vision will be criticised by many, but life is too short to spend time looking over your shoulder at what the other fellow is doing. I don't mind being accused of starting yet another denomination; I don't have a problem with denominations but with the critical spirit behind denominationalism. However, I prefer to think of us as a movement, flexible and versatile. This is much more exciting than living within carefully drawn boundaries. Good fences do not always make good neighbours, especially when they become barriers.

I believe that in this decade, there is a new movement of God in Ireland. The Roman Catholic Church and nominal Protestantism are in decline, and there is a hunger for reality not found in traditional religious institutions. May God make us prepared and willing for the task. I have as big a burden for Cork, Kerry or Galway as I do for towns in the North, but I recognize that cross-cultural missionaries are God's gift. The homogeneous unit principle is that people do not like to cross social, economic or cultural barriers to accept the gospel. If by a Northerner coming to Cork to preach and establish a church, people think they somehow have to leave their Irish identity and heritage behind and cross into a Unionist/British mentality, then they are being asked to do something which Christ is not demanding of them. We must not create obstacles, but recognize people with cross-cultural gifting.

In the summer of 1990, Martin Scott, leader of Cobham Christian Fellowship (now Pioneer People) visited C.F.C. In a prophecy he said that I was pregnant with twins and that, like Jacob and Esau, the younger would rule the elder. He believed that the elder figure represented C.F.C. and after due prayerful consideration, we came to see the church planting vision as the younger brother. We realized that in the future everything would no longer revolve around the Strandtown congregation, rather Strandtown would ultimately serve the vision. This is already being fulfilled as the parent church becomes a resource centre for our new congregations, and on a wider scale through Together for the Kingdom.

As a young believer in the Brethren I was privileged to drive an elderly saint, Tom Rea, to meetings. He had retired from his work as a missionary in Angola where he translated the Bible into several languages. He became my mentor and I hung on his every word; it was like travelling with the Pope. He first went out as a missionary in 1910 at the age of twenty-one. I asked him if on looking back he would change anything? He replied that he would not have gone abroad so young, and added, 'What do you know when you're twenty-one?' In Jesus' day a man could not enter the priesthood until the age of thirty. Even then he was not full-time, but on a rota up to the age of fifty. Jesus himself waited for thirty years to reveal himself as the Messiah. God is not in a hurry. He is looking for maturity as well as availability and a willingness to wait for His time. There is an emphasis at the present on the year 2000. I believe that this is a folly. Let's not focus on a distant date but hear and do what the Father is saying now. We've got to see ourselves in a marathon, not a sprint. In C.F.C. we have deliberately planned our church planting programme to extend to the year 2010 and beyond. I like to take a long-term perspective and engage in effective training and preparation programmes.

During Priscilla's time on the executive committee of the Christian Union at Queen's, the president was David Hepton. He became an historian, and an authority on the rise of evangelicalism in 19th century. During a recent discussion on the subject of church planting as a means of evangelism, he traced previous attempts to spread out into the south of Ireland which had failed. These began with the Methodists in the early 1800s, who aimed to repeat their success on the eastern seaboard of America, in Ireland. At that time the Roman Catholic Church was in disarray and there was no opposition. They believed the time was right, and began to learn Irish in an effort to raise up indigenous churches, but to little effect. In the decades the followed, further fruitless attempts were made by the Moravians, the Brethren and others. 'You need to know,' he concluded, 'history is against you.' There are many on this island who believe that Ireland has no future, only the past repeating itself, and there is little evidence around of a decrease in sectarian attitudes, even within the Church. We have, however, seen sparks of hope ignited through Together for the Kingdom, and look forward to the day when these become a flame. I firmly believe that there are two types of people in religious life. There are shapers and polishers. A polisher takes that which has already been shaped, and applies his gifts to refine and hone. Shapers are those people who bring about change, and create something which did not previously exist. I want to be a shaper, and leave the polishing to someone else. Church planting requires shapers, men and women with pioneering spirit who are sure of their calling and determined to overcome.

We must be prepared to take risks, and adapt as we go. I am all too aware that what I believed five years

PUSHY NORTHERNERS

ago is different from what I believe today, I am under no illusions that I have yet received the whole truth. I don't believe everything God believes, and He doesn't believe everything I believe. I am, however, seeking to live by and follow the light I now have. I have learned to hold all but the fundamentals lightly, so that if the time comes to change, I will be ready. Our God is alive and deals with us on the basis of relationship. No structure or creed can contain Him, yet He chooses to dwell within us. The New Church Movement is only one expression of the Body of Christ, but a vital one for our time. My concern is with getting the job done, and God's revealed means is new churches.

The apostle Paul writes in his letter to the church in Rome, '...from Jerusalem all the way around to Illyricum, I have fully proclaimed the gospel of Christ.' (Romans 15:19) A study of Paul's journeys reveals that he was in the business of establishing believing, Spirit-filled, evangelising churches in these towns. With this as our model, we recognize that Ireland still has a shortfall. Even if every church in the country was full, three quarters of the population would still be unreached and unable to get into a church. It is nonsense to say that Ireland does not need new churches.

What kind of churches are we to plant and how? It is my conviction that a church cannot be built on one man's ministry, whether that be healing, youth work or social action. God has equipped the saints with the gifts of the Holy Spirit, but these cannot be the driving force in church life. Prophecy, God's now word to His people, has a vital part to play in the life of the Church, but I think it is out of balance in many places. You know the sort of thing, 'I had a picture of a three-legged cow in a spotted dress walking on a tightrope, pushing a hippopotamus across in a wheelbarrow.' This is usually followed by a vague, 'I don't know what it means, but I'll leave it with you in love.' The Church always has been, and always will be, built on the Word of God, and it is for lack of teaching that many fellowships flounder.

Throughout my years in ministry, there has been a distinctive shift in the role of charismatic renewal in Ireland. After the initial moves towards reconciliation in the early seventies, and the subsequent diversification into Roman Catholic and Protestant communities, north and south, there is now a new desire to come together. The history of the movement unfortunately demonstrates the ability of its leaders to disagree strongly, as early expectations of the unifying power of covenant relationships have proved unsustainable. However, I believe that a unity based upon mutual respect and the willingness to resolve disagreements is emerging. There is a new focus on the life and teachings of Jesus as a guide to relationships in the Body. He taught his disciples that the greatest in the kingdom is the one who serves. A reinterpretation of how we relate to our brothers and sisters with the emphasis on servanthood, rather than authoritarianism, contributes to harmonious relations with each other and with the evangelical mainstream.

The key word is, restoration, as the birth of new churches, delighting in a freedom from traditional practices, and a movement of some established churches in more charismatic directions, occurs simultaneously. During a decade of charismatic renewal, diversification was inevitable, but new and traditional flavours have again been combined at Together for the Kingdom. A national gathering, no matter how successful, must never become an end in itself. It can however, provide a context for examining existing church structures and honestly facing that which has previously hindered the flow of the Holy Spirit. As we address barriers to progress, personal and corporate, and come together in repentance, we move a step closer to fulfilling Jesus' prayer for unity, among God's people in Ireland.

10

Living with a Limp

As the father of one teenage daughter, and three more in their pre-teens, I have ample opportunity to hear music from the popular charts. Last autumn the group, Simply Red, released a song with the title line, 'I'd give it all up for you.' I listened to the song many times on the radio, and one day I clearly heard God ask, 'Would you?' 'Would I what, Lord?' I replied. 'Would you give it all up for me?' God was challenging my heart and asking if I would still love and serve Him if I did not have C.F.C., if I did not have packed congregations to preach to and the big vision to sustain me.

All too conscious of the past, I pleaded, 'Lord I've done that a couple of times, don't ask me to do it again.' His voice persisted, gentle but firm. I struggled for several days, weeping before the Lord. Finally God reassured me with a wonderful fresh sense that my life was not my own, never mind the church. C.F.C. does not belong to me, the elders or even the people – it is Jesus' church. In the event that He asks me to lay it down, I have the knowledge that He has never abandoned me or my family, and the promise of His continued leading in my life. Times and seasons are in His hands.

Mine is the story of a life rescued from the ashes of failure and despair. In the black period following the resignations, God raised up a man to lead the church into a place where we could receive God's grace in restoration. It just happened to be me, but I am under no illusions that I am here for life. I do believe in strong leadership, but I am not in control.

Years ago I was warned that for Priscilla and me, our greatest stumbling block would be our own competence. I puzzled over this at the time, because I had always thought that God needed gifted, capable people, who were balanced, steady, steeped in the Word, prayerful and righteous. In my early days as a Christian, I believed fundamentally in my need of Christ for conversion, but I managed everything else on my own. As I matured I began to recognize that, although I could deal with most issues, there were times when things got difficult and I became desperate. Then I was forced to pray and was amazed to see God move in supernatural ways.

When God finally revealed to me the full extent of my arrogance, and I humbly acknowledged that Jesus is not only Saviour, but Lord, I began to discover the glorious purpose of God that He should be in control in every area of my life. In exercising personal control not only in my own life, but also over the lives of others, I had put myself in the place where I needed discipline.

The mystery of the gospel for me now is not simply that God uses people whose lives have been broken, but that they are the only type of people He uses! It is when you come to an end of yourself that you discover firstly that you can receive God's salvation, and then that you can be truly used by God. Jesus told His disciples, 'I am the vine; you are the branches. If a man remains in me and I in him, he will bear much fruit; apart from me you can do nothing.' (John 15:5) The most useful people in the kingdom of God are those who have experienced often a crisis, and definitely a process, of learning that without Christ they can do absolutely nothing. The crisis may be one of faith or identity; it may be caused by circumstance or behaviour, but it brings an individual to the place where he says, 'Lord, I cannot go on living, never mind serving you, unless or until I have found your grace.' For many this has required a personal Gethsemane, where a battle has been fought in the will. When we come to the point where we can pray with Jesus, 'Not my will but yours be done,' we are released into the purpose of God for our lives. I have been heard to say of some of our exuberant young leaders, 'They will be fine when they have suffered.' In the Charismatic Movement we have often shied away from the idea of suffering, yet Jesus made it clear that suffering for the sake of the gospel was an integral part of the kingdom of God. We must not confuse the suffering that results from our own stupidity, and that required of us as soldiers in the battle against the powers of Satan. Jesus endured criticism, condemnation and ultimately crucifiction; furthermore He warned us that a servant is not above his master. There are many Christians in this country who have never discovered the fulness of God's grace, because they have not allowed the Holy Spirit to deal with them to the point where they realize the extent of their need.

I have always felt slightly handicapped by the pain of rejection, as a result of my father's desertion of the family. In this area, as with the crises in ministry, the agony of the cure has often seemed worse than the sickness. However, God has undoubtedly used the experiences to reveal my weaknesses, that I might know His strength and communicate the depths of His love to others. In life most of us are coming from or going to a crisis, where God is dealing with the issues of our wills, our hearts and our motivations. Among the most spiritually healthy people I know, are those who have faced such experiences at an early age. At the other end of the scale are leaders who have known over twenty years smooth-running Christian life and service, and have begun to presume on the grace of God. When faced by a crisis they are devastated, and sometimes never recover. It is God's intention that we should reap a harvest of righteousness and peace under His hand of discipline, if we are willing to be trained by it (Hebrews 12:11).

In the same epistle, Paul also writes about the process of shaking, '... the removing of what can be shaken – that is, created things – so that what cannot be shaken may remain.' (Hebrews 12:27) Shaken I most definitely have been, but not shattered. At times when all else was removed, I stood on the love of God. I was not simply clinging on, hoping that my own love for Him would see me through, but I was depending on the vast oceans of His agape love, demonstrated to me at Calvary. I still had the assurance of sins forgiven, and that He held me in the palm of His hand. I knew that He would keep me in the centre of His will, and that I would never be destroyed.

In Ireland, many people have given a mental assent to the teachings of Jesus Christ. The word, salvation, however, means much more than conversion. It is most often used in the New Testament to mean healing or wholeness. To say that we 'were saved' indicates that at a moment in time we met Jesus and accepted him as Saviour. From then we have the knowledge of sins forgiven and an assurance of heaven. It is also correct, however, to say that we are 'being saved,' an ongoing process of sanctification, during which God is changing us into the likeness of Christ. Moreover, one day we will also 'be saved,' when we receive our new bodies, and the things of this earth will pass away. Salvation is not just a momentary experience, but a journey which continues until we are glorified.

Rev. Ken Newell once remarked that in Ireland people are more interested in your birth certificate than in your driving licence. God has given us not only new birth, but equipment for life. There are many people throughout Northern Ireland who insist that they have 'got saved' more than once. Evangelistic meetings and rallies abound, in churches, mission halls and even tents. Hundreds make a decision to follow Christ but discover after days, weeks or months that they cannot 'keep it.' A little boy once asked his mother why he kept falling out of bed. 'Because,' the mother replied, 'you lie too close to where you got in.' Regeneration is only the first step in becoming a follower of Jesus Christ; we are in danger of merely making converts, not true disciples.

I have described myself as a charismatic evangelical. My growing conviction is that evangelicalism, without a dynamic, day-by-day ministry of the Holy Spirit, has little to offer in Ireland. We need people who are not simply born-again, but who are 'being saved' through the power of the Holy Spirit. In many churches there is strong teaching against the ministry of the Holy Spirit, and for others it is a closed book. A growing number of churches, recognizing spiritual dryness, try new systems. They set up home groups, have praise services, introduce modern songs, drama and even interpretive dance. I am absoutely convinced, however, that the key to revival is in the baptism in the Holy Spirit, where the believer is anointed from on high and equipped with power to fulfil God's purposes on earth. While I firmly believe that all the gifts of the Holy Spirit are in operation today, His is a broader ministry which leads us beyond our own efforts into a continuous appropriation of the grace of God.

I have been in great need of God's grace, not only as an individual, but as a leader in a church which was existing in its own strength. The issues that we had to deal with in C.F.C., are issues which I believe face the whole Church in Ireland, and hinder revival, just as they blocked God's blessing in our congregation.

The first of these is the question of control. 'Surely that's what leadership is all about?' some people ask. No, it is not! Paul outlined to the Ephesian church the five-fold ministries of apostle, prophet, evangelist, pastor and teacher and explained their purpose, '... to prepare God's people for works of service, so that the body of Christ may be built up until we all reach unity in the faith and in the knowledge of the Son of God and become mature, attaining to the whole measure of the fulness of Christ.' (Ephesians 4:12) In confessing to and repenting from the sin of control, we publicly handed the church back to Jesus Christ as its rightful head. God raises up leaders in the Body, but He requires that they hold the reigns lightly. It is His purpose that Christ rules through the Holy Spirit.

It is my considered opinion that, like Jacob, Christian Fellowship Church will always walk with a limp, as a constant reminder of God's dealings in our lives. Our association with the Shepherding Movement is not easily forgotten. There are still folk in Belfast who refer to us as, 'the church of the good shepherds,' and even some who perpetuate the rumour that I am permitted more than one wife! For us this is no bad thing, if it keeps us mindful of the grace of God.

I would have to say that I think there are other churches, other groups of leaders, elders and ministers in the country, who also need to come before God in repentance and hand control back to Him. I am not saying that just because we did it others should follow our example, but that God's word to the whole Church is 'let go.' The story is often told of the man who fell over a steep precipice and hung clutching to a branch, which had broken his fall. He shouted for help, 'Is there anyone up there?' A voice from above called back, 'Let go and trust me.' After a pause the cry resumed, 'Is there anyone else up there?' The Church has verbalized, conceptualized and intellectualized Christianity, and is firmly in control, afraid to 'let go and let God.' It is not that we refuse to do it, but that we live in the shadow of generations who have taken the supernatural out of the gospel, therefore abandonment to the Holy Spirit is unfamiliar to us.

In adressing the whole issue of control, the question arises, 'What is the Church?' Our institutions little resemble early gatherings of believers, but rather have become embroiled in secret societies and political affiliation. At the beginning of 1993 the leaders of the four main churches in Northern Ireland made a joint visit to America. It was viewed by many as historic, but one Roman Catholic priest commented on radio, 'They hold immense power, but represent nobody.'

There has been in recent decades, a frustration among ordinary people with the abuse of power by religious leaders. Winds of change are blowing, none more obvious than in relation to the role of women in the Church. In the world in general, and often in the churches, there operates a hidden agenda that men are superior to women. When my third daughter was born, one of my Indian customers in the clothing business was deeply disappointed for me, and suggested a pilgrimage to the Ganges in order to remove the curse! Mentally we assent to 'equal but different,' yet we demonstrate deep prejudice in our lives. When I preach on humility and servanthood in the realm of Christian service it is well received, but in the context of an expression of masculinity, there is often strong resistance. Men wish to retain an outworking of their faith which protects their power but, in the cross, Christ gave up His power in order to achieve our redemption and set an example.

As his Body on earth, God is asking the Church to establish a model which will reflect His heart for society, and this precludes the subjection of women. Perversely, Ireland is a matriarchal society with the mother as the linch-pin, because while men demonstrate power and control, they actually negate responsibility and fail to fulfil God's proper requirements.

In coming to earth as a man, Jesus willingly laid aside the power that was rightfully His, and gave us a model which was a dramatic assault on male privilege. Who but a man could credibly teach and manifest a revolution in relationships by resigning power? In Jesus' day only men had power, therefore it was only as a man that He could show what God was like in the sacrifice of His life for others. At the last supper, when Jesus removed His outer clothing and stooped to wash His disciples' feet, they were astounded. If a woman had done the same thing she would have been ignored. Jesus was restating what maleness is, as he knelt in service and told His followers to do the same.

To the extent to which the Church insists on male dominance and fails to recognize women as valuable and equal in the sight of God, she is impoverished. Men too will find it impossible to discover all that God has for them as they focus on the retention of power. There is a need for repentance, confession, forgiveness and humility so that we serve as whole men and women together.

As a block to the revival of the Church in Ireland, the failure to develop a biblical understanding of power and authority is crucial. The Son of God was the most powerful being in the history of the universe, yet in becoming a man He gave the fullest demonstration of that power. The mystery of the cross is that in becoming flesh and sacrificing His life, Jesus achieved an even greater position of power. In his letter to the Philippians, Paul writes that Jesus did not grasp at equality with God, but humbled himself and became obedient to death, and the passage ends with a shout of triumph, 'Therefore God exalted Him to the highest place and gave Him the name that is above every name, that at the name of Jesus every knee should bow, in heaven and on earth and under the earth and every tongue confess that Jesus Christ is Lord, to the glory of God the Father.' (Philippians 2:9–11) If all the Church does is to imitate the world in its expression of power, through manipulation and the retention of position and place by male superiority, then it is not a question of the Church affecting the world, but the world affecting the Church. Taking Jesus as our example, let us lay down control and operate under a godly authority, which will minister to this land.

11

Worthless Idols

In Ireland, where we have control we need to give it up, where we have power we need to lay it down, and where there is religion, we need to destroy it! I have a friend from Scotland, who was doing evangelistic work in the south of Ireland. He visited Salthill in Galway and was conducting an open-air meeting when he was interrupted by a bystander's shout, 'What do you think of the Irish?' My friend based his reply on Paul's address to the Athenians, 'I see that in every way you are very religious.' His audience took this as a compliment, and certainly a respect for the things of God is a good foundation for society. None-the-less Paul sought to teach the Athenians that the Lord of heaven and earth does not live in temples made by human hands, and Jesus reserved His strongest criticism for those who had a form of religion, while denying its power.

The Irish culture is strongly religious, with many people seeking to earn merit in the sight of God through their own efforts. Northern evangelicals believe fundamentally in justification by faith, but in practice many actually preach and sustain a gospel of works. Once an individual is born again and experiences God's grace, he continues his Christian walk under law, and under a burden of man-made rules and regulations.

Missionaries tell how that at the end of the second world war, they re-entered Japan to find small pockets of young believers. One such group congregated at the local baths, according to Japanese custom, where they prayed together in a communal pool. The missionaries were horrified to discover men and women worshipping God, naked and up to their necks in water. They tried to show their Japanese friends the error of their ways, and suggested that they separate the men from the women. When they returned, they found that the resourceful Christians had stretched a length of string across the middle of the bathing pool, with naked men on one side and naked women on the other! I'm not trying to advocate this practice, but illustrate the foolishness of building a relationship with God on rules and regulations. In his instructions to the Colossians on freedom in Christ, Paul warns believers against being taken captive by human traditions and the basic principles of this world. Most dangerous is their appearance of wisdom and the self-righteousness which can result from their observance. The problem with rules is that they change. Among things considered unspiritual in days gone by, was the wearing of brown shoes and the use of the humble fork. More serious is the effect on those hungry for God, who cannot get past the religious language we use, the clothes we wear, the buildings in which we meet and our forms of worship. We need to evaluate all of these in the light of Scripture, and examine whether having begun with the Spirit, we are now trying to attain the goal by human effort. (Galatians 3:1–5) It is my prayer that our churches in Ireland will be vehicles of grace and love in a torn society, rather than stumbling blocks.

'It is for freedom that Christ has set us free. Stand firm then, and do not let yourselves be burdened by a yoke of slavery.' (Galations 5:1) God is looking for whole people, who have learned to follow the leading of the Holy Spirit in every area of their lives, and who are free to enjoy and use all that He has given to us. Many evangelicals profess to be 'in the world but not of it,' but in practice they are 'of the world' in terms of lifestyle and ambition, but not in it, not involved with real people to influence as salt and light. We have drawn an artificial distinction between the secular and spiritual, that we may protect ourselves from the very people Jesus sought out. His best friends were crooks and fishermen, and He had nothing but reproof for the Pharisees and teachers of the law. Religious and denominational barriers prevent people from coming into the freedom of the gospel. Our devotion must be to Christ alone, so that we are not offering mere ritualism and ceremony. Both sides are guilty and must come before God in repentance.

It is impossible to communicate in words the horror of political and sectarian violence occurring at present in Northern Ireland. Entire communities live in fear and this fuels hatred. Those of us who love the Lord have to find a way to model His new creation, if we are to effect change. In Christ, there is neither Roman Cathlolic nor Protestant, and if we are serious about the establishment of His kingdom in Ireland, we must put to death our religious differences in order to witness the birth of anti-sectarian Christianity. Jesus looked at the heart, and we need an outpouring of the Holy Spirit that we might learn to do the same. As Irishman kills Irishman, many in defence of cold religion, God is calling for those who will stand up and be radical. Reconciliation is impossible in a vacuum, but when religious prejudices are consumed by the fire of the Holy Spirit, from the ashes can rise new life in Christ.

'For He Himself is our peace, who has made the two one and has destroyed the barrier, the dividing wall of hostility, by abolishing in his flesh the law with its commandments and regulations. His purpose was to create in Himself one new man out of the two, thus making peace, and in this one body to reconcile both of them to God through the cross, by which He put to death their hostility.' (Ephesians 2:14–16) One new man in Christ, is our motto for Together for the Kingdom, and we believe that as we lay aside our own religious preferences and prejudices, together we can discover what is on the heart of God for our nation.

We are not despising history, heritage or culture but rather taking on God's perspective.

The coming of Christianity to Ireland through Patrick, introduced a golden age in the 7th and 8th centuries, during which missionaries left these shores to take the good news of the gospel into Scotland, Northern England, Wales and mainland Europe. Ireland became known as 'the land of saints and scholars.' Then through several generations, as invasion followed invasion, Ireland's was a bloody history of seige and rebellion. Time and again the Irish people were victims of other people's greed and domination, and in such an atmosphere, anarchy thrived. The close proximity to Britain made her attentions inevitable, and Ireland struggled to retain an identity of her own. In 1800 the Act of Union abolished the Irish parliament and united the two kingdoms of England and Ireland 'for ever.' In the years that followed, the protection of the Protestant ascendancy status was bound up in the preservation of the Union, while nationalists began to seek its repeal. The Anglo Irish treaty of 1921 saw the establishment of the Irish Free State in twenty-six counties, and the partition of six of the northern counties. Civil War followed, and in 1937 de Valera introduced a new constitution, which named the state, Eire (Ireland), and claimed sovereignty over the six counties. The Northern Ireland parliament sat at Stormont, but was suspended in 1972 when, in the face of continuing political unrest, direct rule from Westminster was introduced. Not content with a twenty-six county Irish republic, the Irish Republican Army (I.R.A.) continues its campaign, with the ultimate aim of removing the border and British rule in the North. Meanwhile parallel atrocities are committed by Ulstermen, in defence of union with Britain.

Our history is dogged with sectarian bloodshed, as violence is used in the pursuit of political ideals. Guilt must be shared by us all, as the prejudices and discriminations of our forefathers have hindered the cause of peace. The Church too must take its share of the blame for the failure to proclaim a non-sectarian gospel, and for perpetuating myths and misunderstandings. However you interpret Ireland's troubled history, it is impossible to avoid the reality that it is one country, politically divided for only seventy-two years. God's love does not recognize borders, and a desire to see our land healed must be on a thirty-two county basis. Mere evangelicalism will never do the job. In Northern Ireland, and even in the corridors of power at Stormont, Protestant evangelicals have signed covenants in their own blood, declaring allegiance to kingdoms other than that of Christ. A new brand of authentic New Testament Christianity is needed, where barriers are demolished, not reinforced.

At the second of our Sunday Night at C.F.C. meetings, a local man, who was an alcoholic, came in about half way through, as we say in Ireland, 'with drink taken.' I was preaching on the Holy Spirit and, in response to an appeal, the visitor made his way to the front of the church. An elder counselled him and led him to the Lord. He was wonderfully converted, and totally delivered from his drink problem. Eventually his wife also came to the Lord, and the couple attended the church for about a year. One night we were praying against the adverse influence of bodies such as the Orange Order, the Black Institution and the Masonic Order in our society. This man took great offence and never returned to fellowship with us, in fact he has become one of our fiercest critics. He left to join a church whose declared desire is to see all of Ireland brought under the British flag once more. Non-sectarian Christianity is not popular in the kingdom of darkness. I believe that Satan operates in the guise of a religious spirit in Ireland; by the power of the Holy Spirit may we recognize and rebuke it.

Undoubtedly we face an enemy intent on destroying the world by setting man against man, woman against woman, man against woman and nation against nation. Behind the physical protagonists in Ireland we need to discern a spiritual power.

'For our struggle is not against flesh and blood, but against the rulers, against the authorities, against the powers of this dark world and against the spiritual forces of evil in the heavenly realms.' (Ephesians 6:12) When Jesus said, 'The kingdom of heaven is at hand,' He was declaring war on the kingdom of darkness. Throughout His life and in His death, He was in confrontation with the devil's dominions. Every time a person was healed, or set free from an evil spirit, it was a pointer to the final defeat of Satan as the kingdom of God advanced. This battle continues to rage today.

The gospels are an account of all that Jesus, 'began to do and to teach.' The book of Acts records that between His resurrection and ascension, Jesus continued to speak and teach about the kingdom of God. The work of redemption at Calvary was completed, finished, perfect, but the establishment of the kingdom had just begun. During his final two years in prison, Paul's preoccupation was to preach the kingdom of God, heralded by the Lord Jesus Christ (Acts 28:31). Paul was declaring the now reign and rule of Jesus through his followers. In His death, Jesus passed the baton on.

To whom then has the baton been passed? Not to a few godly people with an understanding of these things, but to His Body on earth, the Church. The 'called out' people from the world have been given the task of running the last lap.

'His intent was that now, through the church, the manifold wisdom of God should be made known to the rulers and authorities in the heavenly realms, according to his eternal purpose which he accomplished in Christ Jesus our Lord.' (Ephesians 3:10&11) In the gospels, there are two mentions of church. In Matthew chapter sixteen, Jesus establishes the basic, fundamental reality that His Church is built on the revelation of the truth that He is the Christ, the Son of the living God. To believe this, and to submit to His lordship, is the foundation of Church. The first tenet of the kingdom of God is a right relationship with Jesus Christ, then out of this relationship He builds His Church, a new community of redeemed people against whom the gates of hell will not prevail. This is a Body, controlled by Christ as its head, and empowered by the Holy Spirit. To this Body are given the keys of the kingdom and the task of unlocking, and allowing to roam freely, the kingdom of heaven.

As the foundation of the Church is a right vertical relationship between men and God, there follows that its extension operates through right horizontal relationships between men and women in the Body. In communion with God we are so changed that we can begin to express God's love in commuity with one another. Moreover, when things go wrong, we have a means of putting them right. In Matthew chapter eighteen, Jesus teaches about the practical expression of Church as brothers and sisters learn to live out their lives of love. Through the Body of Christ, the powers of darkness are to be defeated and the kingdom of God extended. The Church is God's chosen instrument for bringing in the kingdom in our generation.

This is why the planting of new churches is vital in changing Ireland. It is only through a community of men and women, rightly related to Christ and to each other, that society can be influenced by God's love. We need in every townland, every village, every town, every city, every county and province in Ireland, thousands of such new communities. Many exist, many, many more are needed.

Will we succeed? This is not a dualistic battle being fought between the equal powers of good and evil. Satan is already a defeated foe. At the cross, Jesus disarmed and made a public spectacle of the powers and authorities, and finally triumphed over them! Satan knows that his fate is sealed, but for now he remains the prince of this world. As followers of Jesus Christ, therefore, we live in the now and the not yet. We believe that one day the King will return and usher in His kingdom in all its fulness, but until that day we will continue to work, and pray, 'Your kingdom come.' We must see that final victory by vigorous faith, because while Jesus said that His kingdom was forcefully advancing, He also warned that violent men would attempt to lay hold of it.

The battle ebbs and flows, but final victory is secure. On 6th June, 1944, when the allied armies landed their invasion forces on the Normandy beaches, the war was over and D.Day was declared. However, some of the most vicious and intensive fighting was to follow until V.E.Day, just under one year later. For the Church the victory is settled, but not yet a present reality, so we continue the fight together.

There have been previous revivals in Ireland, but these have been largely confined to the north east corner. In the early 1920s a move of God under the ministry of W.P. Nicholson halted the rising tide of political violence at that time. As the wind of the Holy Spirit blows again across this island, my prayer is that no county will remain untouched by His power to cleanse and restore. Old wineskins will never contain new wine; new structures are necessary, and in Together for the Kingdom we hope to serve this vision.

WORTHLESS IDOLS

Northern Ireland is known throughout the world as a place of political and religious strife. Other nations look on helplessly as political talks fail and opposing factions become entrenched. Innumerable tears have been shed and prayers offered for the people of Ireland. As I travel abroad, I am excited by the increasing numbers of groups meeting throughout the world to pray for us. These prayers are vital in the restraining of evil, and in seeing the purposes of God fulfilled.

Financial aid will never in itself achieve peace, but as we seek to plant new churches throughout Ireland, we are praying for sponsorship for indigenous groups. This is a poor country, proud at times, but quick to recognize genuine commitment to the welfare of its people. Capital projects are necessary, if we are to put down roots in areas previously untouched by the good news of Jesus Christ.

Irish folk do not like to be patronized, but we welcome visitors who come with open hearts and non-judgemental attitudes. If we are to realize our church planting target, then we need manpower. There is plenty of room for everyone. In recent years there have been movements of God in North America, among people from an Irish Catholic background. Our prayer is that God will call some of these Spirit-filled believers to return to Ireland, to work for the extension of the kingdom of God alongside people, with whom they have a natural affinity.

The relationship between the nations of Ireland and England has always been difficult. Many of those who went to the mainland for economic reasons are drifting home. In the north of England, the descendants of the Irishmen who built the roads, railways and canals are experiencing an outpouring of the Holy Spirit, and love is being revived for this suffering country. May God continue to focus the minds of Christians throughout the world on His heart for our small, beautiful island, that Irish men and women may one day worship together in Spirit, and walk together in freedom.

If you would like to know how you can be involved in what God is doing in Ireland, or if you want more information about the work of Paul Reid and the Christian Fellowship Church, please write to:

> Christian Fellowship Church
> 173 Holywood Road
> Belfast
> **BT4 2DG**